D1706314

SPIKE MILLIGAN'S
THE
MELTING POT

SPIKE MILLIGAN'S — THE — MELTING POT

Written by
Spike Milligan and Neil Shand

Illustrated by
Bill Tidy

Robson Books

FIRST PUBLISHED IN GREAT BRITAIN IN 1983 BY ROBSON BOOKS LTD.,
BOLSOVER HOUSE, 5-6 CLIPSTONE ST., LONDON W1P 7EB. SCRIPT COPYRIGHT
© 1983 SPIKE MILLIGAN AND NEIL SHAND. ILLUSTRATIONS COPYRIGHT © 1983
BILL TIDY.

British Library Cataloguing in Publication Data

Milligan, Spike
    Spike Milligan's The melting pot
    1. Melting pot (Television program)
    2. Television plays
    I. Title   II. Shand, Neil
    791.45'72   PN1992.77.M/

    ISBN 0-86051-195-2

Printed in Hungary

The Melting Pot was recorded for BBC Television in 1975, with Roger Race as the producer. The permanent cast was as follows:

MR VAN GOGH	*Spike Milligan*
MR REMBRANDT	*John Bird*
PADDY O'BRIEN	*Frank Carson*
NEFERTITI SKUPINSKI	*Alexandra Dane*
LUIGI O'REILLY	*Wayne Brown*
ERIC LEE FUNG	*Harry Fowler*
RICHARD ARMITAGE	*John Bluthal*
SHEIK YAMANI	*Anthony Brothers*
COLONEL GROPE	*Robert Dorning*
BLUEY NOTTS	*Bill Kerr*

Other characters appeared on a temporary basis from week to week.

Characters

MR VAN GOGH | an illegal Pakistani immigrant
MR REMBRANDT | Van Gogh's son, also an illegal immigrant
PADDY O'BRIEN | an Irish Republican landlord and coalman
NEFERTITI SKUPINSKI | O'Brien's voluptuous, South African-bred daughter
LUIGI O'REILLY | a black Yorkshireman
ERIC LEE FUNG | a Chinese cockney spiv
RICHARD ARMITAGE | an Orthodox London Jew
SHEIK YAMANI | an Orthodox Arab who speaks with a Scots accent as he's been learning banking at the Bank of Scotland, Peckham
COLONEL GROPE | an ex-Indian Army, alcoholic racialist
BLUEY NOTTS | an Australian bookie's clerk, a crude racialist

EPISODE
1

1

Scene 1 *A deserted beach somewhere in the English Channel. Heavy sea mist. Occasional call of a seagull. Sound of fog horns, and throb of a ship's engine. An anchor is dropped. Sound of Pakistani voices talking answered by a gruff cockney.*

COCKNEY   This is the place.

VAN GOGH   What place, please?

COCKNEY   England.

VAN GOGH   England? I do not see any England.

COCKNEY   Well, it's — er — been rainin' 'eavy.

VAN GOGH   What position are we over?

COCKNEY   Piccadilly Circus.

Out of the mist looms a rowing boat. It grinds onto the beach. We see an elderly Pakistani and his son, both wearing ill-fitting European suits and trilby hats.

VAN GOGH   This is the Piccadilly Circus?

COCKNEY   Yeah.

VAN GOGH   Where are the animals?

COCKNEY   No, it ain't that kind of circus, it's a sort of shopping area.

VAN GOGH   Then where are the people?

COCKNEY   Well — er — it's early closing, isn't it?

The cockney picks up two suitcases and hurls them onto the beach, where they split open revealing various Indian paraphernalia, like brass cooking pots, puggarees, etc.

COCKNEY   There you are, all ready for English Customs.

VAN GOGH   I don't like these customs.

REMBRANDT   On behalf of my father and I, we thank you for bringing us to the land of freedom, truth and honesty.

COCKNEY   That'll be five hundred nicker.

VAN GOGH   Five hundred knickers?

COCKNEY   Pounds.

VAN GOGH   At the start you said one hundred.

COCKNEY   I know, but while we have been coming there's been inflation, hasn't there?

The Pakistani hands over £500.

COCKNEY   Ta. Now then, you walk inland until you get to a big highway. Now, remember the secret sign. (*He gives the hitch-hiker's thumb sign.*) Don't tell anyone else, or they'll all be doing it.

⚙

Scene 2   *M2 motorway, pouring with rain. The two Pakistanis stand soaked, holding split-open suitcases.*

REMBRANDT   What did he say about the transport?

VAN GOGH   He is telling us that we show our thumbs and that when a lorry stops that is the one he is arranging for.

They both do the hitch-hiker's sign. Lorry after lorry passes them, drenching them even further with spray. Finally a pantechnicon pulls up with a coal-black driver. He leans out of the cab and speaks with an astounding Eton accent.

DRIVER   Where are you chappies going?

REMBRANDT   We want to get to Brixton, the land of the free.

DRIVER   Er, yes, you ought to do well there.

REMBRANDT   You are English?

DRIVER   Yes.

REMBRANDT   You've had a good summer then!

They drive off. On the back of the lorry we see: 'GIOVANNI BAPTISTI'S YORKSHIRE PUDDING LIKE MUM MAKES'.

✿

Scene 3   *Brixton street market. The pantechnicon with the two Pakistanis draws up at a bus stop. The queue is entirely made up of immigrants, mostly black.*

DRIVER   Right, chaps — here we are.

REMBRANDT   Is this still England?

DRIVER   Oh, yes.

VAN GOGH   I am glad that you told us, I would never have known.

The driver hurls their suitcases down and they hit the pavement and split open again. They laboriously re-pack them and, looking up, they see a sign: 'LEW HAMBURGER: TURF ACCOUNTANT'.

VAN GOGH   Good heavens! What a bit of lucking. A hamburger shop.

REMBRANDT   Good, just what we need to practise our European eating on.

✿

Scene 4   *Interior of betting shop. Usual crowd of miserable, impoverished punters. By a loudspeaker an old, ragged punter listens intently to the racing results. Lying on the filthy floor, face downwards, another drunken punter*

clutches his betting slip. A very tough Australian bookie's clerk's phone rings. The Australian snatches it up, says 'Piss off', and hangs up. He spots the two Pakistanis.

BLUEY   Yes?

VAN GOGH   Have you got beans on toast?

BLUEY   (*Turns and looks at the race board.*) No, no beans on toast.

REMBRANDT   Well, what have you got then?

BLUEY   Well, there's Chico's Special, Lucky French, Caesar's Choice, and a new joint favourite, Hello Sailor.

VAN GOGH   What would you recommend?

BLUEY   You can't go far wrong with Chico's Special.

VAN GOGH   Alright, Chico's Special twice.

BLUEY   Oh? You want it each way?

REMBRANDT   We'll have it any way.

BLUEY   (*Making out betting sheet.*) One Chico's Special at five to four.

VAN GOGH   Five to four? My God, we can't wait that long.

REMBRANDT   Please, what is a Chico Special?

BLUEY   What do you mean? It's a horse, mate, can't you read? (*Points to board.*) Two-year-old Stakes.

VAN GOGH   You are selling two-year-old steaks made from horses' meat and then you expect us to wait until five to four before we can eat them?

BLUEY   (*Absolutely baffled.*) What the bloody hell are you bungs talking about? 'Ere, you're on bloody drugs, aren't you?

VAN GOGH   No, we are not on drugs, we are on Social Security.

BLUEY   Ah, yes, you bloody Poms, y're all the same.

VAN GOGH   We are not bloody Poms, we are from Amsterdam.

An argument breaks out among the three of them with much shouting. The Pakistanis back out and walk over the drunk in the middle of the floor. The phone rings and Bluey shouts 'Piss off' down it and hangs up.

✿

Scene 5   *Night-time in the sleaziest part of Soho, London. Endless sound of various discos. Police sirens. Series of large photographs outside a strip joint. Each photograph shows a woman with a huge bosom. In each photograph the bosom gets progressively bigger. The Pakistanis arrive, holding a piece of paper.*

VAN GOGH   (*Reading.*) Meet me outside the Big Pussy Club, 13 Dean Street, at 8 o'clock. Bring the money. Signed, Lord Haversham, Home Secretary.

REMBRANDT   Ah, yes, this is the place.

Van Gogh's eyes take in the first photograph.

VAN GOGH   Oh dear, oh dear, oh dear. (*He then moves on to the second pair of boobs. He says in a louder voice*) Oh dear, oh dear, oh dear, another one. This must be the place for poor nursing mothers who have no means of support.

REMBRANDT   Please do not look at them, Father. Remember what the doctor said.

From a dark doorway a very scruffy spiv watches the approaching Pakistanis.

SPIV   Psst! Psst!

The Pakistanis see him and go across.

SPIV   Aah — are you the two wogs from Amsterdam? I am your contact.

VAN GOGH   Lord Haversham?

SPIV   Yes, the Home Secretary. 'Ave you got the lolly?

VAN GOGH   Yes, five hundred pounds in unmarked sterling with the Queen's head on, God bless her.

SPIV   (*Snatching the money.*) Yes, God bless 'er. Now, 'ere's your passports and an address to stay at. Just say Dick sent you.

REMBRANDT   Dick? Pardon me, Dick, if you are the Home Secretary, why are you doing business in a doorway?

SPIV   It's 'er, Mrs Thatcher, she's made a lot of cuts. She should have done them on 'er wrists.

VAN GOGH   Oh, what is a Thatcher?

SPIV   It's a sort of death wish. That is, we all wish she were dead. Now, my fee for this introduction will be —

Police siren approaches. Spiv runs off. A policeman rushes past with a truncheon.

✿

Scene 6   *Night-time. Street sign: Piles Road, WC1. Sound of distant drunken singing, tin can being kicked. Howling of tom-cats. Sound of explosion. Drunken singing stops. Taxi draws up. Out get the two Pakistanis. Taxi driver chucks their cases out. They hit the pavement and split open again.*

TAXI DRIVER   This is it. That will be sixty-three pounds.

VAN GOGH   Sixty-three pounds for one mile?

TAXI DRIVER   Yer — it's inflation.

VAN GOGH   (*He hands money across.*) Can we have a receipt?

Taxi drives off. Rembrandt looks at street sign.

REMBRANDT   Ah, this is the street, Piles Road, WC1.

VAN GOGH   Only one WC for the whole road?

REMBRANDT   No, no the WC is for the postman.

VAN GOGH   The postman? Then where do *we* all go?

All the while they are walking until they arrive at No. 7.

REMBRANDT   Ah, here we are: No. 7. Remember that we are not wogs, we are from Amsterdam.

VAN GOGH   Don't forget to say that *Dick* sent us.

REMBRANDT   (*Practises saying it.*) *Dick* sent us ... Sick dent us ... No, no *Dick* sent us ...

VAN GOGH   Oh, are *you* going to say Dick sent us?

REMBRANDT   Yes, *I* will say that Dick sent us.

VAN GOGH   Alright then, *you* say Sick dent us, no, *Dick* sent us.

The door opens. Standing there is a Junoesque, large-bosomed, very shapely sexy female in a mini-skirt. She speaks with a South African accent.

VAN GOGH   Good evening, Dick, guess who sent us?

REMBRANDT   Madam, good evening. He means, Dick sent both of us.

NEFERTITI   Are you are the two kaffirs — er — Dutch gents from India, yes?

REMBRANDT   Yes, I am Rembrandt and this is my father, Van Gogh. Real Dutch names.

NEFERTITI   Oh yes. He hasn't chopped his ear off yet, then? I am the housekeeper, Nefertiti. I'll show you to your rooms.

She starts to walk upstairs, followed by Van Gogh lugging the suitcases. She displays large amounts of stocking-top and lingerie which considerably affects Van Gogh.

VAN GOGH   Oh dear.

NEFERTITI   Are your bags too much for you?

VAN GOGH No, yours are. (*He collapses face downwards and slides down the staircase like a corpse.*)

✿

Scene 7 *A squalid attic room. Bare boards. Peeling wall-paper. Two bunks with sordid mattresses. A light bulb hangs from the ceiling. Against the wall is an outline of what used to be a WC and which is now removed; however, the cistern is still hanging over the wall and the water pipe from it appears to run into the next room. Above the blocked-up fireplace is a ghastly picture of Ghandi, pinned to the wall with a six-inch nail through his forehead. A large po is under the bunk bed. The door opens. Nefertiti leads the two Pakistanis in.*

NEFERTITI Our PR Department told us that you were holy gurus and you wanted your room emptied of all the corrupting symbols of Western decadence, except for the po. I put this picture of Ghandi here to cheer you up. You have heard of Ghandi?

VAN GOGH Not lately.

NEFERTITI Well, if there's anything you want in the night, let me know.

She exits. They both look around the room, a bit dejected.

VAN GOGH Well, it's better than nothing. (*He pauses.*) No, wait a minute, it isn't.

✿

Scene 8 *Front room of No. 7, Piles Road. Appalling '30s decor. Seated at outsize dining-table covered in newspapers is Paddy O'Brien. He is black, owing to his work as a coalman. Nefertiti enters.*

NEFERTITI Oh, Dad, you're home early tonight. Did they drop charges?

PADDY No, no, sold out of coal. The Electricity Board bought it — they found it cheaper to have coal fires than electric ones. Did the wogs arrive?

NEFERTITI Yes, I have put them in the Winston Churchill Suite.

Scene 9 *The attic room. The time is a few hours after the arrival of the Pakistanis. They have unpacked, and the room is now littered with brass cooking pots, odd clothes hanging up on nails, a brass statue of an Indian many-armed god on the mantelpiece, and a couple of 1945 demob suits.*

REMBRANDT   My God, Bapu, do you have to put that up? (*Indicates god.*) We don't want these people to think that we are praying to an octopus.

VAN GOGH   Oh dear, oh dear. My own son denying his own god. I know I never should have sent you to a Christian school. You went in a fully-fledged Hindu and came out a failed Catholic.

REMBRANDT   Tell me, *why* did you allow them to make me a Catholic?

VAN GOGH   Because immediately they reduced the fees by half and you didn't have to stand outside the classroom and learn your lessons through the window.

REMBRANDT   Yes, believe me, the Catholic Church has very good business organization.

VAN GOGH   I will tell you why. Their God is Jewish. J. Christ & Co. Limited, branches everywhere.

The door opens and an Arab (Sheik Yamani) in full costume walks in and pulls WC chain in the room.

YAMANI   (*Scottish accent.*) Excuse me, lads, it's nae my idea of fun. (*He exits.*)

Van Gogh squats on the floor to attend to some of the brass bowls. Nefertiti enters with a cup of tea in each hand. She observes Van Gogh squatting.

NEFERTITI   Ah, ah, ah, ah — you are not allowed to do it there.

REMBRANDT   He is only squatting.

NEFERTITI   Not in this bloody house, you don't. You pay rent and you have to give it to me once a week. Now, there's a few rules in this house. No pets or women in the rooms after July 6th. (*She exits.*)

REMBRANDT   We have to organize a new lifestyle now, Bapu. You will do the cleaning and the cooking, the shopping and the laundry, the beds and po. I will do everything else.

VAN GOGH   There *isn't* anything else.

REMBRANDT   I must go out and make our fortune in one of the following: asset-stripping, off-shore investments, holding companies, pornographic magazines, blue films, and I will start tomorrow.

VAN GOGH   Where?

REMBRANDT   Brixton Labour Exchange.

✪

Scene 10   *Morning: the communal bathroom. Three wash-basins with cracked mirrors over each. Victorian bath in corner in which sleeps a Jamaican. Suspended above him in a hammock is another Jamaican by whom is a sign in illiterate handwriting: 'To let during daylight hours — apply occupant'. At one sink Paddy the coalman is about to wash. He is coated in coal-dust. Enter Van Gogh with brass pots.*

VAN GOGH   Hello, Mr man, sir. You are having a jolly good wash, toodle-pip.

PADDY   Oh, you've learnt the language, then?

Paddy washes himself, removing all the black. Van Gogh looks up and sees the transformation.

VAN GOGH   (*Screaming.*) No, no, no!

Jamaican falls out of hammock into bath below. Van Gogh runs out, screaming.

✪

Scene 11   *The attic room. Rembrandt is in his bunk reading* Exchange and Mart. *He is wearing a pair of brand-new pyjamas. He is still wearing his trilby hat.*

REMBRANDT   One hundred per cent Bri-Nylon, non-inflammable. No artificial

flavour added. Do not smoke in bed. Keep out of reach of children. In event of skin rash, consult a doctor. British-made in Taiwan.

In rushes Van Gogh.

VAN GOGH   You must never use the soap here!

REMBRANDT   What is the matter with the soap?

VAN GOGH   It is racial soap.

REMBRANDT   Racial soap?

VAN GOGH   Yes. I saw a black man washing with it and I watched his nationality coming off and go down the plughole.

Scene 12   *The attic, later. Van Gogh is getting into the lower bunk, and Rembrandt is getting into the top bunk.*

REMBRANDT   Do you want the light out?

VAN GOGH   No, I am reading my pyjama label. Listen to this. 'Use these pyjama before April 3rd 1984, thereafter the manufacturer cannot be held responsible for any accidents that take place inside this garment.' You see how well they look after their people here?

REMBRANDT   Yes, it's the Welfare State — from the womb to the doom.

VAN GOGH   Tell me, why do they have one bed over the other?

REMBRANDT   It's the English class system. The upper class up here and the working class down there.

VAN GOGH   Ah, yes — if a wild animal gets into the room, it eats the working class first.

REMBRANDT   (*Reading* Exchange and Mart.) Ah, listen: 'For sale: one pair Riviera

shoes, property of a gentleman. Sturdy 1922 style, only done 13,000 miles. Reconditioned laces, as new. Owner going to South Africa while there is still time.'

VAN GOGH   Oh, that is good. I will go there first thing in the morning. (*As he talks, the black man runs into the room, pulls the chain and exits.*)

✿

Scene 13   *Daytime. Exterior of house in a quiet street in Wimbledon. Name on gate is 'Poona', written large. At a bay window appears the middle-aged, red-faced, retired Indian Army Colonel Grope, dressed as though he has known better times. He is sipping his morning gin and tonic when suddenly a look of horror comes over his face. He has seen Van Gogh approaching in bare feet and carrying a Union Jack Harrods carrier bag.*

COLONEL   My God, Molly, there's a wog coming up the garden path.

He disappears from the window as Van Gogh walks up the drive towards the front door. He is halfway there when a double-barrelled shot-gun appears out of the letterbox, accompanied by the Colonel's voice.

COLONEL   Get out of my garden, you Indian swine! We had relatives in the Black Hole of Calcutta.

VAN GOGH   I am not from Calcutta, I am from Brixton.

COLONEL   Well, we've got relatives in that black hole as well.

The Colonel fires both barrels, which explode Van Gogh's carrier bag, releasing a great cloud of flour and an outpouring of uncooked rice.

VAN GOGH   Please stop. I am from Amsterdam and you have injured my dinner. I have come about the shoes, toodle-pip!

Immediately the demeanour of the Colonel changes. The gun barrels are withdrawn. There is a stifled sound from behind the door, then it opens.

COLONEL   You have come to buy the Riviera shoes?

VAN GOGH   (*Referring to piece of paper.*) Property of gentleman, laces as new.

COLONEL   Yes, yes, but have you got money?

VAN GOGH   Yes.

COLONEL   With the Queen's head on?

VAN GOGH   Yes, and a little bit of the neck.

COLONEL   Ah. I will go and get them.

Van Gogh goes to follow him in but the Colonel turns.

COLONEL   No, no! You mustn't come inside, my wife's — er — er — a leper.

He closes the door. There is a pause. He reappears in his socks holding the shoes he was recently wearing. The shoes are a good size 13, very bulky and wide-footed.

COLONEL   There you are, then. I've been warming them for you. That will be eight pounds.

Van Gogh sits on the doorstep with the shoes in front of him.

COLONEL   What are you doing, man?

VAN GOGH   (*Putting the shoes on.*) First I must road test them for safety.

Van Gogh then does a series of strange walks up and down the street followed by a sock-footed Colonel.

COLONEL   Look, man all this isn't necessary — they have only done 13,000 miles, they are still under guarantee.

VAN GOGH   They look like retreads to me, sir.

COLONEL   Nevertheless, they are still under guarantee, I tell you. My wife did last year's marathon in them.

VAN GOGH   Now I must see how they corner.

Van Gogh does a series of cornerings, leaning inwards as though on a motor bike.

COLONEL   That's it, as you are, right hand down, there now . . . that will be nine pounds.

VAN GOGH   You said eight pounds.

COLONEL   Inflation.

VAN GOGH   One more test: jumping.

Van Gogh runs and jumps over a garden wall. There is the death howl of a cat as he lands on it. Van Gogh bends down and picks up dead black moggy by tail. An awful woman appears at an upstairs window.

WOMAN   You bugger, you have killed my Nigger!

An argument breaks out between Van Gogh, the Colonel and the woman. A black police constable appears on the scene.

CONSTABLE   (*Very refined voice.*) Now then, who has killed a nigger?

✿

Scene 14   *Daytime: the attic room. Van Gogh alone in room cleaning the shoes. The door opens and Rembrandt appears in a bus conductor's uniform.*

REMBRANDT   Look, Bapu, look. At last I have made it.

VAN GOGH   (*Looking at uniform.*) Yes, my son, it looks as if you've made it. What Regiment have you joined?

REMBRANDT   The Royal London Passenger Transport Board.

NEFERTITI   (*Voice off.*) Dinner's ready.

ONE CARELESS OWNER..

Scene 15   *The hideous front room of No. 7 Piles Road. The large table on one side of the room is laid for dinner. All the other occupants of the boarding-house are seated around it. They are: the landlord, Paddy; the Australian bookie, Bluey Notts; the cockney Chinaman, Eric Lee Fung; the black Yorkshireman, Luigi O'Reilly; the London Jew, Richard Armitage; and the Scottish Arab, Sheik Yamani. Nefertiti is ladling out various foods. They are all watching a large TV which is in the corner of the room. The two Pakistanis enter.*

NEFERTITI   These are our two new lodgers, Mr Rembrandt and Mr Van Gogh — they're from Holland.

ERIC FUNG   If they're from Holland, I'm a bloody Chinaman.

PADDY   Well, you are a bloody Chinaman.

ERIC FUNG   Ah, yes, I am a Chinaman, but not *recently*. You see, it's like Darwin's revolution of the species. In time these features will change — I mean, my great-great-grandson could end up looking like Robert Redford.

BLUEY   Wait a minute, you are the two bungs who wanted to eat the winner of the 3.30.

REMBRANDT   Yes, it was all a misunderstanding.

Nefertiti is now pouring some soup into the Pakistanis' plates which they proceed to cut up with a knife and fork.

YAMANI   You need to use yer spoon, laddie.

VAN GOGH   Oh, thanking you. What job are you doing over here, then?

YAMANI   I came here to study English. I am a cashier at the Bank of Scotland. It's very nice here. Mind you, I'd give my right arm to be back in bonnie Libya.

RICHARD   (*Strong Jewish accent.*) Right. Someone give me a chopper, I'll send the bugger back.

They go for each other.

PADDY   Here, here, none of that, now. You know it says in the lease tenants will not kill each other at the dinner table.

RICHARD   No . . . we leave that to the bloody grub, don't we?

VAN GOGH   (*Watching the television.*) Is that the evening news?

PADDY   No — it's 'Kojak'.

VAN GOGH   Oh yes, 'I'm Alright Kojak'. The Peter Sellers film.

PADDY   Oh, Christ! He's a *New York Detective.*

VAN GOGH   He is very bald.

PADDY   Well, he shaves his head you see.

BLUEY   And I will tell you why. He *was* bald.

VAN GOGH   If he is bald, why does he shave his head when there isn't anything there?

BLUEY   Ah, well, there's those wispy bits that hang round the sides. Now, he happens to see this other bloke with the shiny nut — what's his name — Yul Brynner. Now, he had *all* those bits hanging around, but he was *clever* — he shaved them all off and he varnished his head. And since he did, they booked him to play 'Anna and the King of Siam', so Kojak sees that and he copies it.

VAN GOGH   But if you shave all the wispy bits off, that makes the bald balder.

BLUEY   *We* know that, but what Yul Brynner and Kojak did was circulate leaflets saying that they had lovely thick heads of curly black hair, but they shaved it all off to look more rugged.

YAMANI   Oh. Why then don't they just wear a bald wig in the first place?

VAN GOGH   The first place? You mean there's more than one place you can stick a bald wig on?

PADDY   For Christ's sake, will you shut up? I am trying to watch this bloody show. Kojak is just going to kill the nigger.

LUIGI O'REILLY (*Yorkshire accent*.) Ah, ah, ah, less of that nigger talk.

PADDY   Right then, Kojak is going to kill the lovely coloured gentleman who has just split his wife's head open with a bloody meat-axe.

They all stare at the screen for a while.

YAMANI   Oh dear, look at the size of his hooter, he must be Jewish.

RICHARD   Why because he has a big conk does he have to be Jewish? Look at Paul Newman — he is Jewish — he hasn't got a big conk.

YAMANI   That's because he has had a nose job.

RICHARD   Nose job, my foot.

VAN GOGH   Is that right — you can have a nose job on your foot?

PADDY   Will you all *shut up*! I can't hear 'Who loves ya baby'!

He turns up the volume on the television. Immediately there is a loud banging on the wall behind the TV and a German voice says:

GERMAN   Please in zere will you please make turning down ze television — zere are people in here trying to sleep.

Richard rushes across the room and hammers on the wall with his ear to it.

RICHARD   Shut up, you German swine! With consciences like yours, how can you bloody sleep?

The picture falls off the wall onto Richard's nut and renders him unconscious. General argument.

Scene 16 *Midnight: same front room. The table has been cleared. The diners are now sleeping on it, covered by blankets. Paddy is sitting on the sofa with the two Pakistanis. The late news is on:*

NEWSCASTER ...Mrs Thatcher said she is going to hold down prices of petrol at eight pounds a gallon. Now the weather.

WEATHERMAN There will be heavy gales around the coast, high gales inland and there will be strong winds and hail, frost and snow. So, have a nice weekend. That's all for tonight. Goodnight.(*Sound of 'God Save the Queen' being played over television picture of Queen on horseback, trooping the colour.*)

VAN GOGH Ah good, there's a new film starting starring a North-West Mounted Policelady wearing a red Mountie coat.

PADDY Dat's the Queen.

VAN GOGH Can't she afford a car?

REMBRANDT I know that tune...

PADDY Dat's the National Anthem.

Both Pakistanis stand and sing 'God Save the Queen.'

EPISODE
2

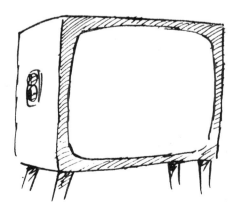

2

Scene 1 *The bathroom at No. 7, Piles Road. The three sinks are blocked and full of water. Near the sink is a bed with two black Jamaicans asleep. Both wear woolly hats with bobbles on the top. The bed has blankets and two overcoats as well; above it hangs a line of washing. Dressed in the suit he always wears, Van Gogh is standing in the bath, facing a large geyser which is steaming. He is attempting to wash his pyjamas, but the geyser only occasionally squirts water. This is accompanied by an earthquake-like shuddering, with great rumbling and bubbling noises. The steam envelops the two sleepers. Van Gogh tries to gather the water in the bucket. Above him is a hammock in which sleeps another man.*

VAN GOGH   My God, this is supposed to be a hot water system. (*Reads the geyser.*) Made by Thomas Crapper, 1889. (*Geyser vibrates.*) All it does is three squirts an hour. I can do better than that, and they are charging me and my son £18 a week, share bathroom, no women in the room or near offers.

JAMAICAN   (*In bed.*) Please to be keepin' quiet, me an' ma chauffeur am tryin' to get some sleep.

VAN GOGH   I wouldn't let my daughter marry one of them.

Geyser starts to shudder. Van Gogh rushes to collect the hot water.

REMBRANDT   (*Enters with a bucket of water.*) Bapu? Are we still blocked up?

VAN GOGH   Yes, they are fully blocked, as advertised in the *Evening News*.

REMBRANDT   Then it will have to go down the loo.

VAN GOGH   There is no light in here.

REMBRANDT   Don't worry, I've done it in the dark before. (*He opens WC door and empties bucket.*)

BLUEY   (*Stifled sound from WC, then he appears clutching soaked trousers.*) You bloody drongo...

REMBRANDT   I apologize.

BLUEY   Apologize, my arse.

REMBRANDT   Very well, I apologize to your arse.

VAN GOGH   You should have kept the door shut.

BLUEY   Shut? With no window in 'ere? I've 'ad enough. There's too many bloody abos in this country. (*Starts to exit.*) I'm gonna see about my return passage.

VAN GOGH   Is that blocked up too?

JAMAICAN   (*In bed.*) Fo' de secon' time, man, we'se tryin' to sleep.

REMBRANDT   What is that lot, Bapu?

VAN GOGH   They are the British Leyland night shift.

REMBRANDT   If I was that colour, that is the shift I'd work on.

VAN GOGH   My God, I been here two hours and only got half a pyjama done. (*He holds up bottom half of pyjamas, the colours have run and the garment is a mess.*)

REMBRANDT   Are you using Rizzo? With the added Dronkalite extra blue granules, 2p off? (*Sings.*) Washes whites whiter.

Geyser starts to shudder. Enter a very hairy, arrogant cockney plumber, chewing gum.

PLUMBER   Are these the ones that are blocked up? (*Indicates basin.*)

REMBRANDT   Ah, yes. (*Points to basins.*) There.

The plumber smashes the outlet pipe of all three basins. Water gushes to floor.

PLUMBER   Twenty-eight pound.

REMBRANDT   The landlord is downstairs.

PLUMBER   Downstairs? That'll be twenty-eight pound, plus four pound stairs money. (*Exits.*) That'll be thirty-two quid...

Geyser goes mad, issues forth masses of steam. Van Gogh reacts. Hammock collapses and Jamaican occupant falls into bath among Rizzo suds – he comes up white.

✿

Scene 2   *The attic room. A transistor radio is pouring out disc jockey crap music, commercial break gunge. Rembrandt is completing his toilet, looking into a mirror, the surface of which is warped and cracked. He has plastered his hair down, 1935-style.*

REMBRANDT   May I have the pleasure of the next foxtrot? Oh yes, my family have been foxtrotting for years. My dear young lady/gentleman, can I get you a jam sandwich or shall I play the concertina? My father owns the Bank of Dublin; how many millions will you inherit? Will you marry me, everything is in working order. (*He is in the process of tying his tie, cutting a piece of white cardboard or paper to the shape of a breast-pocket handkerchief, when there is a knock on the door.*)

NEFERTITI   Can I come in?

REMBRANDT   Just a minute. (*Picks up aerosol, squirts jacket armpits.*) Come in.

Enter Nefertiti. She carries a bundle of newspapers.

NEFERTITI   I've come to put fresh newspapers in your drawers. (*She sniffs. Picks up aerosol can.*) Oh? Fly killer.

Rembrandt grabs it and looks at the label in surprise.

NEFERTITI   Oh. By the way (*she reaches inside her bra to remove a piece of paper.*) I've got to show you this... (*She can't find it.*) Funny, it was there a moment ago.

REMBRANDT   It's still there by the look of it.

NEFERTITI   (*Finds it.*) Ah. Mr O'Brien asked me to give it to you, it's the receipt for last week's rent, and he says, can he have it?

REMBRANDT   Don't worry, we will be drawing our supplementary benefit this afternoon.

Enter Van Gogh. The trousers of his suit are now a dirty bleached white from the mid thighs down. He is literally steaming.

VAN GOGH   That bloody Rizzo.

NEFERTITI   It's got bleach in it.

REMBRANDT   Those cost £1.30 in the Oxfam sale.

NEFERTITI   (*Looking closely at the trousers.*) You could dye them.

VAN GOGH   They are already dead.

NEFERTITI   Look, can I speak plainly to you stupid kaffirs?

REMBRANDT   Well, you can't speak plainer than that.

Hammering on wall. Van Gogh runs and pulls the chain on cistern. It flushes WC which is in the next room.

NEFERTITI   Look, you can take all these crappy clothes to the laundromat and wash the lot for 60p. Or if you like, I'll burn them in the garden for nothing. Oh, my God, the lunch. (*She rushes out.*)

VAN GOGH   (*Noticing receipt which Rembrandt is holding.*) What is that?

REMBRANDT   It is a recipe for the rent.

VAN GOGH   Good. At last we'll know how to make it.

✪

Scene 3   *The front room. Seated around the table are the lodgers. Nefertiti is putting plates of food in front of them. Rembrandt bangs his lamb chop on his plate, which breaks.*

PADDY   God Almighty, Nef, what have you done to these cutlets?

BLOODY RIZZO

MINT SAUCE
PLATE
FIXATIVE

NEFERTITI   (*Very calmly, continuing to serve burnt food.*) I'll tell you what I've done (*bursts into tears*) I've burnt the bloody things. It's that bloody North Sea Gas.

VAN GOGH   In India we cook on cow dung.

PADDY   Well, we don't have any North Sea cow dung here.

VAN GOGH   It is more economical. You just stand behind the cow and wait.

PADDY   Look, *wogs* may cook on cowshit — we don't.

VAN GOGH   Wogs — okay, but we are British wogs and we must not be confused with Indian wogs...come, my son. We must go to the (*reads a card*) Laundarama, 239 Terrible Street, Peckham, closed Wednesdays, nearest tube Uxbridge, buy a Red Rover and save one third on a Awayday with Jimmy Savile.

LUIGI O'REILLY   (*Black Yorkshireman, speaking with mouth full.*) You tell 'em, Ram Jam. You bloody Micks, come over t'ere to save 'emselves bein' blown up over there, then start layin' down t' law to people like me — Yorkshire born and bred.

PADDY   It must have been brown bread. You wasn't a chip off the old block, you was a slice off a black pudding. (*He bursts out laughing.*)

LUIGI   Go on, laff, you slit-eyed twit...You're one of the Chinese noodles they forgot to take away.

Eric stands up; he has tablecloth tucked into his shirt. It spills dinner.

PADDY   Stop all this, now. Look, Mr Rembrandt, I'm sorry; I apologize for calling you and yer Dad bloody wogs.

REMBRANDT   You didn't say *bloody*.

PADDY   Well, I'm sayin' it now: *bloody wogs*. I'm sorry. You are British subjects, like Luigi O'Reilly of Yorkshire, Eric Lee Fung of Battersea, and Mrs Nefertiti Skupinski, née O'Brien, late of Johannesburg, who married a Polish RAF pilot who had become British so that she could become English.

VAN GOGH   What?

PADDY   Of course, the Yid and the Gypo here, now they *are* bloody foreigners.

YAMANI   I'm nay a Gypo...the blood of Mohamet runs through my veins.

RICHARD   And I bet it runs backwards, like your army.

YAMANI   Shut up, Sheenie.

RICHARD   Sheenie. If you were any kind of an Arab you'd be on the Golan Heights trying to work out the instructions on yer Chinese rocket-launcher.

REMBRANDT   I would...

YAMANI   Listen, Jew — if Hitler was alive today I'd ask him to make me a gauleiter.

PADDY   From what I hear, he couldn't even make a cigarette lighter.

REMBRANDT   I'm trying to say, my father and I accept your apology. Now, we go to the laundrette, for a good 60p.

Van Gogh empties burnt dinner into carrier bag.

PADDY   You gonna post that to Bangladesh?

✪

Scene 4 *Outside an Oxfam shop. Sounds of traffic cacophony. Aeroplane goes overhead. Drills. Distant sound of the 'Happy Wanderers' on radio. A very ragged World War Two hero, bedecked with medals, is selling matches from a tray with a Union Jack hanging down. He wears a blind man's glasses.*

MAN   Matches... British Toyota matches... only 80p a box plus VAT — £1.20.

Van Gogh and Rembrandt arrive, both carrying their Union Jack carrier bags. One is full of laundry. They read an advert in the window of the Oxfam shop.

REMBRANDT   Please help. Fifty million Indians are starving.

WAR HERO   (*Corner of mouth.*) Let the bastards starve. Matches. British matches ...as used by the British as central heating.

Scene 5   *Inside Oxfam shop. Behind the counter is a lady of great breeding. A mass of charities and garden fetes written on her face, she is about fifty, gushing, totally useless. She wears a Laura Ashley gown, a large straw garden party hat, and a hearing aid. The control is attached to her bosom, wire runs to her earpiece.*

WOMAN   (*She is already talking as Van Gogh and Rembrandt enter.*) Ahhh, how nice, how *very* nice of you to help like this. I'm afraid Lady Mitworth-Handleigh isn't here today. She is in Southall doing wonderful things for the black deaf.

VAN GOGH   You hear that? They've got Black Death in Southall.

WOMAN   You'll have to speak up, my hearing aid is jammed.

VAN GOGH   (*To Rembrandt.*) What's wrong?

REMBRANDT   Someone has put jam on her hearing aid.

The woman fiddles with the control which oscillates, then we hear a commercial for Capital Radio coming through loud and clear.

WOMAN   Capital Radio is up the road, dear.

VAN GOGH   We don't want Capital Radio...

WOMAN   What?

VAN GOGH   (*Shouts.*) We don't want Capital Radio.

As he is speaking, two Japanese tourists come in, a man and woman. They stare at the shouting Pakistani.

JAPANESE   Excuse, is this Buckingham Palace?

VAN GOGH   (*Shouts.*) No, it isn't.

JAPANESE   Ahso. (*Exits.*)

REMBRANDT   And Ahso to you.

Colonel Grope comes in, buttoning up his brown overall, on the pocket of which is a Union Jack with the words: Oxfam Voluntary Worker.

WOMAN   Ah, Colonel Grope, I'm so glad...

COLONEL   I'm a little late, my dear...I lost the bottle opener...

WOMAN   I must fly, I'm late for my 'Cosi Fan Tutte'.

COLONEL   Yes, yes, off you go, Fanny. (*Still looking down, buttoning his coat, unaware of Van Gogh and Rembrandt.*) Now, gentlemen, what can I — (*He looks up. His demeanour changes. Pre-recorded voice of Colonel saying: 'Wogs.' Roll of drums at execution. Pre-recorded voice of Colonel saying: 'Forty years ago I'd tie them to the mouths of cannons and...' Sound of cannon blasting off. Devilish grin spreads over his face.*) Now, what do you want?

VAN GOGH   (*Shouts.*) We have been told that...

REMBRANDT   *He's* not deaf.

COLONEL   Who said I was?

VAN GOGH   We are told that you feed starving Indians.

COLONEL   Yes, but we don't serve the food here. You have to go to Calcutta, lie on the pavement and hold up one withered arm with a tin.

Pause as Van Gogh and Rembrandt lay the burnt food out in front of the Colonel.

COLONEL   Very interesting, but what is it?

REMBRANDT   Dinner. (*Waits.*)

Pause.

COLONEL   I didn't order dinner.

REMBRANDT   It is not for you, it is for the people of Calcutta, lying on the pavement, holding up the withered arm.

VAN GOGH   Yes, they can put it up their tins.

As he talks, devilish look appears on Colonel's face. Pre-recorded roll of drums, distant bugle, voice of Colonel saying: 'Forty years ago I'd tie 'em to the mouths of cannons and...' Cannons roar; screams.

Scene 6 *Interior of washeteria. Sign announcing in gothic script: 'Ye Old English Washeteria. Proprietor: Duncan Skupinski. Registered as an oil tanker in Liberia. Travellers' cheques encouraged. Treble Green Shield Stamps'. Beneath it another garish-coloured sign: 'With every 60lb wash free give-away set, one plastic champagne glass, complete'. The Manageress stands behind a plastic counter, giving washing powder to an Arab woman in purdah.*

MANAGERESS   Don't eat it, darlin' — puttee in machinee.

PURDAH WOMAN   (*Gruff cockney soldier's voice.*) I know what I'm bleedin' doin . . . it's this or the glass-house.

The washeteria is totally foul and grotty. The machines are worn out, some scorched and blackened. On several there is aerosol spray grafitti. Empty fag packets, old beer cans and newspapers are scattered about floor. A drunk is sprawled face-down, groaning and muttering. The customers consist of two Sikhs, a Ghanaian in traditional dress, a very tweedy middle-aged English lady in a two-piece suit, two London Jamaicans (fat ladies) in European dress, a Hindu lady in a sari, and two very Italian-looking Soho-types (male). As the purdah lady leaves, Van Gogh and Rembrandt approach. The Manageress has a small TV set on the counter facing her. An aerial cable snakes over it, through an adjacent door or window.

MALE VOICE   (*From outside, somewhere high above.*) Is that any better, Rita?

MANAGERESS   (*Looking at set.*) No . . . it's shaky . . . Reginald Bosanquet's wig is sliding off his nut.

REMBRANDT   Pardon me, sir.

MANAGERESS   Sir? Cheeky bugger. I suppose the sexes all look alike to them. Wot you want, Ram Jam, a curry?

REMBRANDT   No, we want to do our laundry.

MANAGERESS   Where is it?

REMBRANDT   He is wearing it.

MANAGERESS   He can't get into my machines wearing it, the paddles will beat him to death. (*Pause.*) He doesn't look as if he's long to go anyway.

VAN GOGH   I only want to do the suit.

MANAGERESS   He'll have to strip off. 'E's wearing something underneath, isn't he?

REMBRANDT   Oh yes, he's got plenty underneath...

MALE VOICE   (*From above.*) Wot's on now, Rita?

MANAGERESS   'Crossroads'. (*To Rembrandt*.) That's me old man, he's on the roof, fixing the aerial. It won't work down here. It's these English sets — crap. We can't afford a Japanese one.

MALE VOICE   (*From above.*) Wot's it like now?

MANAGERESS   (*Pouring powder out for Van Gogh and Rembrandt.*) It's the commercial. There's a tart fast asleep in a posh bed... with water crashin' on the rocks. (*Pours more powder — pause.*) Now there's a geezer in black, divin' off a yacht... Ooh — 'e's killed a shark...

MALE VOICE   (*From above.*) 'Ow?

MANAGERESS   'E's broken its bleedin' neck. Ooh. Saucy devil, 'e's climbin' up a rope with 'is teeth... (*Hands Pakistanis powder and drops voice.*) That's yours, darlin'... and that's yours — 60p each.

They put money down. She takes the money, puts it in the till, then tears off Green Shield Stamps, reaches under the desk, and hands them each a very nasty plastic champagne glass.

MANAGERESS   That's yer champagne glass, darlin'.

REMBRANDT   Champagne? Oh!

MANAGERESS   Now the geezer in the black's come leapin' through the tart's window and 'e's putting somethin' on her bed.

MALE VOICE   (*From above.*) What is it?

MANAGERESS   (*She raises her voice.*) A roll of kazi paper... 'Pink Magic... the perfect gift from a stranger'.

MALE VOICE   (*From above.*) 'As he left 'is card? How!

MANAGERESS   Machine number nine... that's the one with the door still on.

Van Gogh and Rembrandt sit next to the tweedy English lady who is reading The Times. *She holds* The Times *up between herself and the Indians as a defence.*

VAN GOGH   Ah, number nine — doctor's orders.

REMBRANDT   (*Takes Van Gogh's glass.*) I will hold it until they bring it round.

VAN GOGH   Fancy, they are serving champagne in laundries. That's the benefit of going into the Common European Market. (*Starts to take his suit off.*) Yes, we did a... (*low gasp of horror from tweedy English lady*) ... good thing leaving the Calcutta gutters.

Van Gogh removes suit, starts to stuff it into machine. The door falls off but he manages to get it back. Rembrandt throws the powder in rather dramatically. Van Gogh puts in entire box of Rizzo. He is now in outsized long underwear and long-sleeved vest. He has his long johns on back to front. The tweedy English lady with The Times *is slowly tearing a small hole in the page to spy through. Occasional gasps of horror issue forth. Distant sounds of 'Crossroads' on the telly. Van Gogh switches the machine on.*

VAN GOGH   I think this was made by Thomas Crapper, too.

From his Union Jack carrier bag Rembrandt takes out a banana and starts to eat.

REMBRANDT   (*Looks up.*) Isn't it wonderful, in this country, electric light in every room.

VAN GOGH   In Bangladesh we had oil lamps in every room.

REMBRANDT   We only had one room.

VAN GOGH   And we had an oil lamp in it.

REMBRANDT   So?

VAN GOGH   So we had an oil lamp in every room...

WE HAD AN OIL LAMP...

PEEPING TOM A[...]

..AND A BANANA IN EVERY ROOM!

A very smart guardsman enters holding hands with a delightful gay boy. The gay boy wears flared red corduroys, sleeveless body vest, a pink ostrich-feather boa. They are holding hands and carrying laundry bags. The gay wears an Afro wig which he removes and puts in the washing machine. He sits back with the guardsman, to the amazement of Van Gogh and Rembrandt.

GUARDSMAN   Wot you starin' at? It's legal now, isn't it?

The tweedy English lady is now missing. Sound of police siren approaching. Several customers rush to hide behind machines. A coloured Jamaican constable enters with six-foot trainee police cadet. He has an Alsatian on a lead.

MANAGERESS   Hello, come in for the dropsy, 'ave yer?

CONSTABLE   We had a 'phone call from a lady.

TWEEDY LADY   (*Comes in.*) That was me, officer.

CONSTABLE   You complained about a case of indecent exposure.

MANAGERESS   A flasher, was there? 'Ave I missed it?

TWEEDY LADY   That's the man. (*Points to Van Gogh.*)

Manageress immediately searches him with her eyes. Constable and dog handler stroll around the back of Van Gogh, who is now standing. He revolves with them.

CONSTABLE   This lady has accused you of gross indecency and flashing.

VAN GOGH   Rubbish. I was born like this.

CONSTABLE   Why aren't you wearing any clothes?

VAN GOGH   They are in the machine.

CONSTABLE   I'm sorry, Madam, there seems to be a mistake. Are you sure you haven't been seeing things?

VAN GOGH   If she was, it wasn't mine.

Sound of breaking glass from street. Screams. Pistol shots. The policeman, cadet

and dog rush off, followed by Manageress. The tweedy lady groans and faints to the floor. Rembrandt runs out after the police. Sound of an affray, with police whistles. Police dog growling, ripping cloth. Van Gogh is left with the fainted tweedy lady.

VAN GOGH   She has fallen face down. I must give her artificial insemination. (*Gets across her back and starts to carry out vigorous massage.*) I shouldn't be doing this. Someone from the National Health should be pumping.

TWEEDY LADY   Oooohhh...ooohh...

VAN GOGH   Alright, missy, you'll soon be home.

The manageress comes back in, sees a compromising situation.

MANAGERESS   'Ere, stop that. No shaggin' in my laundries. (*She picks up a bucket full of starch and water and throws it over them. Immediately the washing machine starts to smoke.*) My machine. You haven't been putting bloody curry in there, 'ave you? 'Ow long you had it on?

Van Gogh looks at his wrist — his watch is missing.

VAN GOGH   My watch. My wrist has been mugged.

MANAGERESS   Police. Police. (*Exits.*)

TWEEDY LADY   (*Sits up behind Van Gogh.*) Oohhh, a black one.

She faints again. Van Gogh gives more artificial respiration. Rembrandt rushes back in. He has been in a punch-up. His right trouser leg is in shreds.

REMBRANDT   Bloody police dog...trained in Brixton.

Washing machine explodes. The manageress throws another bucket of starch over Van Gogh as she re-enters. Black constable enters. His trouser legs are shredded. Sound of barking, off. Policeman and Rembrandt immediately leap up on top of washing machine.

CONSTABLE   Look out, he's not properly trained.

REMBRANDT   You think I don't know that?

Police cadet re-enters, crying, with dog.

CADET   (*Sobbing.*) I can't control him, Sarge.

CONSTABLE   (*On walkie talkie.*) Hello? Can you send in a net and two pounds of raw meat to the laundromat? Hurry.

MANAGERESS   Arrest that coon for damaging my property.

Drunk stands up singing 'Life is a cabaret, oh chum'. To his amazement, he is now covered from head to foot in white starch.

✿

Scene 7   *The front room of No. 7, Piles Road, late at night. Rain is seeping through the ceiling. Around the room is a mixture of buckets, jugs, tin baths. The floor is covered with newspapers to absorb the damp. There is a saucepan on top of the piano. The TV is on with an umbrella on it. All the occupants are there except Van Gogh and Rembrandt. Paddy is just walking from the table to the TV.*

NEFERTITI   (*Mending socks on the couch.*) How in God's name do you get such big holes in your socks?

BLUEY   I'll tell you how, he wears 'em as a balaclava.

PADDY   Look at this, race riots *in Golders Green.*

RICHARD   (*Leaps up from table where he has been using a hand adding-machine.*) Golders Green: my property, my property. (*He rushes to set.*)

YAMANI   (*At the table, writing a letter home.*) Property? What you got there, a crematorium?

RICHARD   You fascist. Jews don't burn their dead in Golders Green.

YAMANI   Only because it's a smokeless zone.

RICHARD   (*Wags finger.*) One day, one day you'll run out of oil. Then back to the camels.

BLUEY   Will you two bungs shut up. Y're ruining 'Blankety Blank'.

RICHARD   (*Staggered*.) How could *anything* ruin 'Blankety Blank'?

BLUEY   You should take this lot and do what we did with the Abos, bung 'em up North.

PADDY   North? That's Scotland, what in God's name would they do?

LUIGI   They'd bloody eat 'em, wouldn't they?

Sound of police siren approaching. Stops outside. Car doors slam. Paddy leaps to his feet, switches off TV, pulls a white cloth over it, places a crucifix on top, kneels and chants in Latin. All the others kneel as well. The lounge door opens, in comes the black constable.

CONSTABLE   Good evening. I'm sorry to interrupt the service, Father.

PADDY   What TV set, Officer? I—

CONSTABLE   One of your lodgers has had an accident.

PADDY   I know nothing about a TV set, Officer.

The door slowly opens and Van Gogh and Rembrandt walk in. Van Gogh has gone stiff with starch. He walks stiff-legged, supported by Rembrandt.

PADDY   Good God, where have you been — the sales?

VAN GOGH   The laundry. The woman is fainting and I am trying to give her artificial insemination.

PADDY   Oh dear—

REMBRANDT   And they are throwing a bucket of starch over him.

PADDY   Get him on the dinner table.

VAN GOGH   My God — they're going to eat me.

PADDY   Don't be bloody silly. Get a hammer — I'll try and break him down.

Meanwhile all the lodgers are carrying the stiffened Van Gogh and laying him on the dining table. They ad lib under the dialogue.

REMBRANDT   Get his legs.

LUIGI   Mind the jam.

PADDY   Get his hat off.

ERIC FUNG   Don't get the bread knives up his jacksie.

PADDY   (*Hammering Van Gogh with a wooden mallet*.) Don't worry. You'll be able to claim sick benefit.

The table collapses. From the TV we hear the news.

NEWSCASTER   Another bomb has exploded in the House of Lords toilet. Max Byegroul gets an OBE. More clues have been uncovered in the Nude Vicar Murders . . .

EPISODE 3

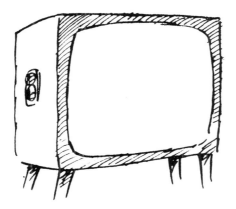

3

Scene 1   *The front room of No. 7, Piles Road: tea-time. Strung across back of room are washing lines full of ragged underwear...the occasional female garment dividing them. Paddy is seated in the armchair in front of the TV. His feet are in a bowl of water, which is standing on a sheet of newspaper. He has a mangy, stuffed terrier on his lap. He is pushing back the stuffing from the seams and taping over the holes with Elastoplast. He has a mug of tea balanced on TV set. Nefertiti is at the table laying out various odds and ends of food from the sideboard. The electric kettle starts whistling as it boils on the sideboard. Richard Armitage enters wearing a black trilby hat. He takes off the hat and hangs it on the back of the door, revealing a white Jewish skullcap. He begins to read the* Jewish Chronicle.

RICHARD   Anything good on TV?

PADDY   Yes — my tea! Ha!

RICHARD   (*Reading.*) I see a Golders Green lady died and left £900,000. Pity...it doesn't say *where* she left it.

PADDY   You cannot take it with you.

RICHARD   Not with this Government, you can't!

PADDY   Turn the TV sound up.

VOICE FROM TV   However, Mrs Thatcher said it wouldn't do women any good even if they did leave the light on. The Home Office say Britain now has a healthy lead in unemployment, beating Poland by 2.5 million.

RICHARD   You know, if Mr Begin ran this country he'd soon have it on its feet!

PADDY   Well, we haven't got far to go — we're on our bloody knees already.

...SHE DIDN'T LEAVE THE MONEY HERE EITHER!

UNEMPLOYDARITY

In comes Sheik Yamani, carying plastic Union Jack shopping bag. He puts down umbrella.

RICHARD   Ah...the return of the Red Bladder! The John Hanson of Brixton Market and failed oil sheik of 1980.

Yamani puts carrier bag on table and starts to rummage around in the bottom of the bag.

YAMANI   Did you know — if all the Jews were laid end to end, the fun I'd have with a steamroller!

RICHARD   Oh funny. Who said the Arabs have no sense of humour?

PADDY   Everybody!

Sounds of thunder and lightning. In come a soaked Van Gogh and Rembrandt.

VAN GOGH   Good evening. Isn't it terrible weather? Is it just in the South East?

PADDY   No, it's all over.

VAN GOGH   It's all over me. (*He shakes his umbrella.*)

NEFERTITI   That's right, shake it all over the bloody floor.

VAN GOGH   Oh. Thank you.

REMBRANDT   Oh dear...my poor plates of feet.

PADDY   Tired out after a hard day's queueing at the labour exchange?

VAN GOGH   It is not our fault!

REMBRANDT   No. I went for a job as an assistant accountant. As soon as they see I am coloured they say I am not tall enough.

VAN GOGH   Yes, if he'd been white he'd been tall enough. I went for a job as doorman at the British Museum. When they saw me they said, 'Can you speak Latin?'

YAMANI   Latin's a dead language.

VAN GOGH   That's why I didn't get it! I wasn't dead!

NEFERTITI   I'll say he's not dead. *You* try passing him on the stairs.

PADDY   I can't see what pleasure he'd get passing *me* on the stairs.

The kettle whistles on sideboard. It sounds like Trimphone. Van Gogh answers the phone.

VAN GOGH   Hello?

NEFERTITI   It's the kettle! (*She grabs phone from Van Gogh and replaces receiver*.)

VAN GOGH   What is that animal you are shining with boot polish, Mr O'Brien?

PADDY   It's an old family pet who passed on. She died of deafness.

VAN GOGH   Died of deafness?

PADDY   Yes, there was this steam roller coming up behind and she didn't hear it!

VAN GOGH   Oh dear.

PADDY   When she died we had her stuffed . . . come to think of it, she had quite a bit of that while she was alive.

Richard Armitage goes over to the TV set and turns up the volume.

VOICE FROM TV   Finally Israeli planes bombed and strafed Arab bases on the Syrian border for more than thirty minutes.

Yamani goes to shake Richard, but stops.

RICHARD   It's not enough — with the money we sent them they can afford bombing for hours.

Yamani goes to attack him again. Eric Fung enters. He, too, is soaked.

ERIC FUNG   Gawd! What a day — not one bloody winner — not even a place. I'm going to emigrate. (*Smashes hand down on table — a fork flies up in the air*.)

VAN GOGH   (*Reading a 'kids' comic*.) What is straight and never comes back? An Irish boomerang.

SYRIAN BORDER STRAFED OR MONEY BACK!

I'M PAYING FOR PEOPLE TO FLY THAT HIGH!

Paddy laughs.

VAN GOGH   Why is that funny?

PADDY   Because it is!

VAN GOGH   I didn't see it. There is an Irishman with a straight bit of wood, yes? He throws it and everybody laughs.

PADDY   You see, Ghandi, our humour is razor-edged, we're very quick. The only time your lot ever laughed is when we left India.

ERIC FUNG   And a right bleedin' mess they made of it.

VAN GOGH   Rubbish, it has never been better in India.

PADDY   Then why did you come over here?

VAN GOGH   To get our own back!

PADDY   You've all come over here because youse all got the arse out of your trousers — no — worse, youse got your arse out of *someone else's* trousers.

The phone rings and Van Gogh switches the kettle off – realizes it's the phone.

VAN GOGH   Hello? What? What colour knickers am I wearing? I—

NEFERTITI   It's for me. (*She takes phone, slams it down*.) He was early today.

PADDY   Who was?

NEFERTITI   My obscene phone caller.

PADDY   How long's this been going on? Have you told the police?

VAN GOGH   Surely the police don't want to know what colour her knickers are?

RICHARD   See? They just *don't* understand our language.

YAMANI   *Our* language! Look who's talking! In Israel, if they couldn't wave their hands (*he does it*) around in the air nobody would understand a word they were saying.

VAN GOGH   It is natural to wave the hands about.

ERIC FUNG   Don't you start. The only thing your lot wave about has given you a population of six hundred million.

VAN GOGH   (*To Paddy*.) Is that Chinese or English sense of humour?

ERIC FUNG   *I am not a Chinese* — I am a London cockney!

VAN GOGH   Then why, when you are out of the room, *he* (*points at O'Brien*) is saying 'Where's that bloody Chinkiepoo?'

ERIC FUNG   Because he's a bloody racialist.

PADDY   I'm not a racist. Now, quiet for the footy results. (*Sound of TV*.) I suppose those Proddy bastards have beaten Celtic again.

VOICE FROM TV   Celtic 0, Rangers 7.

PADDY   (*Throws his newspaper down*.) Oh God. They must have crippled the goalie...

VAN GOGH   Why should the Catholics always win?

PADDY   Because they're *holier*. They burn candles.

VAN GOGH   Celtic burn candles?

PADDY   (*Very devout*.) Oh yesss...

VAN GOGH   And the Rangers?

PADDY   (*Shouts*.) They burn the bloody stands down.

Eric Fung spots Arab paper-wrapped bottle. Yamani unwraps it.

ERIC FUNG   Brown ale? I thought you Arabs didn't drink?

Yamani snatches it back.

RICHARD   That's right, it's against his faith.

YAMANI   But there's nothing in the Koran to say you shouldn't buy a bottle, provided you empty it.

Strains of 'Coronation Street' opening music from TV.

VAN GOGH   'Coronation Street?' Time for bed.

PADDY   (*Looks at watch.*) It's only half past bloody seven.

VAN GOGH   All my life, I believe 'Early to bed, early to rise, make a man healthy, wealthy and wise'.

PADDY   (*Looks him up and down.*) What went wrong?

NEFERTITI   (*Bringing Paddy a mug of tea with large shamrock on it.*) Why don't you two go out and mix with some *real* English people for a change? Go to the pub in Peckham — they let kaffirs in there. The Queen's Arms.

REMBRANDT   Yes, that's a *good* idea, Bapu!

VAN GOGH   They don't like coloureds in the saloon bar.

NEFERTITI   Rubbish, remember London isn't like Capetown.

PADDY   It bloody soon will be...

LUIGI   In this country you don't have to worry about some bugger like Christian Barnard following you in an ambulance.

NEFERTITI   Listen, kaffir, thanks to Christian Barnard, quite a few people have lived *several* hours longer than they would have.

PADDY   Don't give us that. We know for a fact at night time there's hundreds of these bloody white doctors hiding in shop doorways waiting for the drunken niggers to go by and then — bong! They belt them on the back of the head with a shovel — and before they hit the ground, they've got their heart, liver and lungs all in a plastic bag and into the fridge.

NEFERTITI   That's a vicious rumour spread by the kaffirs when they came round.

REMBRANDT   Very fine then, Mrs Nefertiti. We will take your advice and go to the pub. Come, Bapu.

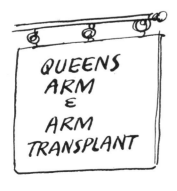

Scene 2 *Van Gogh and Rembrandt are eating fish and chips at head of a bus queue. There is a litter bin attached to the bus stop. It is brimming over with rubbish. Van Gogh empties some out so he can put his own in. He turns to man in queue.*

VAN GOGH   Keep Britain tidy, man.

MAN   If you want to keep Britain tidy — *go home!*

VAN GOGH   Very good, where do the English catch fish and chips?

REMBRANDT   Iceland. It's very difficult.

VAN GOGH   Why?

REMBRANDT   The English ship has to ram the Iceland ship, and they throw fish and chips at them.

VAN GOGH   (*Reading paper.*) Look what the print says: Mark Phillips has fallen off his horse at Badminton.

REMBRANDT   See? Their royalty can afford to play badminton on horseback.

Sound of an approaching drunk singing 'If I Ruled the World'.

VAN GOGH   (*Looking up at numbers on bus stop.*) London Passenger Transport is a very fine thing.

REMBRANDT   Especially the way Pakistan is running it.

VAN GOGH   Yes, in India, we had to walk four miles to the village.

REMBRANDT   We had to walk four miles to this bus stop.

VAN GOGH   That is why you are fifty pence better off.

REMBRANDT   Fifty? I only started with forty.

VAN GOGH   See, you didn't have enough money anyway.

REMBRANDT   (*Reads bus numbers on board.*) Twenty-three, one-two-nine, seventy-six, fourtee.

DRUNK   (*Now in the queue.*) Bingo!

VAN GOGH   Bingo?

DRUNK   (*Breaks into song.*) Life is a cabaret, oh chum!

Policeman walks into the scene. He addresses himself to the drunk.

POLICEMAN   Pardon me, sir, are these foreigners threatening you?

DRUNK   No.

POLICEMAN   Are you *sure*, sir?

DRUNK   Sure — bugger off!

Policeman looks disappointed and exits.

VAN GOGH   Ah, here comes the bus.

Bus drives straight past without stopping. But the drunk disappears.

REMBRANDT   And there it goes.

A second bus passes immediately. Drunk reappears in queue.

REMBRANDT   If it goes on like this we'll soon be able to go by taxi.

✿

Scene 3   *Outside the Queen's Arms. Newspapers litter the pavement. Several windows in the pub are cracked and held together with sticky tape. From inside come very rowdy noises. Sound of till going almost continuously. There is a group of German tourists singing world war two marching songs. There is pop music from a juke box with people joining in. A drunk comes staggering out through the door, on which are stuck a few tattered posters announcing events like Irish Hooley Night, Greek Bicentennial Dance at Peckham, Lesbian Rally. A big dog is tethered outside. A man comes out and puts pint of beer in front of him.*

Bus goes by without stopping. When it's gone Van Gogh and Rembrandt are revealed clutching each other.

VAN GOGH   My God — they don't give you much time to get off here.

REMBRANDT   Did you ring the bell?

VAN GOGH   I didn't have one.

REMBRANDT   It was a bloody white driver. See? They are taking our jobs away. Ah, this is the pub. The Queen's Arms.

They go into the pub.

❂

Scene 4   *Inside the Queen's Arms. Bluey Notts is behind the bar.*

VAN GOGH   Ah, hello, R. Australian Bluey Notts. Is this the Queen's Arms?

BLUEY   Yes.

VAN GOGH   Can we speak to her, please?

BLUEY   And we've had all those jokes before. The Manager's name is Nickolas Minniepolies. He's in Greece.

REMBRANDT   Why? Is he going rusty? Ha ha!

BLUEY   We've heard that one, too! He'll be back in three weeks.

VAN GOGH   We can't wait that long!

BLUEY   Look, I haven't got all bloody night.

REMBRANDT   This is a free house?

BLUEY   Yes.

REMBRANDT   We'll have two free drinks.

BLUEY   Free house means you can sell any kind of beer as long as you're not tied to a brewery.

ALL THE BEST

VAN GOGH   We have to be tied up to a brewery before we can get a drink?

BLUEY   You have to pay for yer drinks — p.a. *pay*.

REMBRANDT   (*Crisply*.) P.a. is not pay ... p.a. is *pa*.

BLUEY   Alright then, you have to *pa* for your bloody drinks.

VAN GOGH   What *is* he talking about?

REMBRANDT   He says we have to pa — to pay — for our drinks.

VAN GOGH   Two glasses of water.

BLUEY   (*Gritting teeth*.) We don't serve water on its own. (*Leans across bar*) You gotta have something with it.

VAN GOGH   A box of matches.

Bluey breaks a glass.

Enter Colonel Grope. He is wearing plus-fours, and a white fedora tied with string to his lapels. He has his arm in a sling.

Bluey is now going mad.

BLUEY   You've got to have an alcoholic drink with it.

VAN GOGH   Why an alcoholic drink with a box of matches?

Pause.

BLUEY   May I make an alternative suggestion?

VAN GOGH   What?

BLUEY   Piss off.

COLONEL   How *dare* you insult these visiting Eastern potentates.

VAN GOGH   We are not ...

COLONEL   (*To Van Gogh.*) Shut up, you black bastard. (*To Bluey.*) You, a mere colonial, bowing and scraping to those bloody huns (*points and raises his voice and faces them*) who fought against us in the last war. (*Turns back to Bluey.*) And then you vent your spleen upon these poor miserable wogs.

Bluey tries to pull the Colonel across the counter. Colonel's lapel comes off.

BLUEY   Listen, drongo, I fought on your bloody side. We left Australia undefended to hang on to Tobruk; while we was doing that you pommie ponces was showing the white flag to the nips in Singapore—

COLONEL   It was a triumph for British washing powders.

GERMAN   (*Approaching bar.*) Sieben pilsners and schnell!

BLUEY   (*Shouts.*) We haven't got any schnell, you ignorant bastards. (*Normal.*) Now, 'ave you two bungs made up your bloody minds?

COLONEL   (*To Pakistanis.*) Let me help you, gentlemen. The law insists you have alcohol with your water. Your religion says no. Let me make the supreme sacrifice for your heathen gods — you drink all the water, I'll drink the acolohol. (*To Bluey.*) Four double brandies.

REMBRANDT   We are very grateful to you.

COLONEL   Not as grateful as I am to you. (*Aside.*) If you can't get rid of 'em, bankrupt them.

Rembrandt passes brandy to Colonel.

COLONEL   Chin chin. Bottoms up.

VAN GOGH   Chin chin, up your bottom.

Scene 5 *Outside the Queen's Arms. The tethered dog is whining – his glass is empty. Man comes out with a refill. A blind old ex-serviceman in dark glasses is selling matches from a tray. A Union Jack hangs from the front. Policeman approaches.*

From inside the pub we can hear German marching songs sung by the tourists. The noise level is rising. The till never stops. Occasionally a glass breaks.

MATCH-SELLER   Matches . . . buy British matches, help beat the recession. Genuine British Toyota matches.

POLICEMAN   Come on, move along, no soliciting in the street.

Match-seller raises his glasses. Complete change of demeanour.

MATCH-SELLER   I'm not a solicitor! I'm a . . .

POLICEMAN   You know the deal — one pound cash or a murder charge.

MATCH-SELLER   (*Passing him a quid.*) It used to be 50p.

POLICEMAN   Inflation! (*He empties match-seller's money from tin mug, into his own pocket.*) It's tax-deductible.

✿

Scene 6 *Inside the pub. The Colonel, Van Gogh and Rembrandt are seated at a table loaded with empty glasses, full ashtrays, empty crisp packets. The Colonel is drunk.*

COLONEL   (*Pouring.*) The Colonel is drunk. Have another water . . . have it on me!

VAN GOGH   No, no, I'm sorry, I cannot drink any more.

COLONEL   One for the road.

VAN GOGH   Any more, and I'll be doing it on the road.

REMBRANDT   Ahhh! (*Gets up and runs out.*)

VAN GOGH   See what I mean?

COLONEL   (*Shouts after Rembrandt.*) Hold it!

VAN GOGH   He knows he has to hold it.

COLONEL   I'll go and see if there's any messages down there for me. (*Exits.*)

An old woman of sixty is sitting at bar. She is nearly toothless. A failed lady of the streets, she sets her eyes on Van Gogh. She gets up and walks across to him.

WOMAN   'Ello, you handsome Sepoy.

VAN GOGH   I'm not a Sepoy. I'm Mr Van Gogh of England.

Pulls out passport.

WOMAN   You remind me of my late husband.

VAN GOGH   Oh, he's late. Is he working overtime?

WOMAN   Wot are you doin' of later tonight? (*She nudges him and winks.*)

VAN GOGH   Not you for a start. No! I will go home and watch Angela Rippon on TV.

WOMAN   Turns you on, does it?

VAN GOGH   No, *you* have to turn *it* on.

WOMAN   'Ow'd you like to come back to Houndsditch and I'll give you a pelvic massage?

The Colonel returns with bright red lipstick kiss on his cheek.

COLONEL   God, it's not even safe in the Men's.

Wipes off kiss with handkerchief.

REMBRANDT   (*Runs in, very shaken.*) Oh, what a terrible experience — there was a man in the WC with *no arms*! He asked me if I was a boy scout.

COLONEL   (*Looks at woman.*) Who is this ex-boxer?

WANT A RELIEF MASSAGE WITH A PENSION BOOK?

VAN GOGH   This man wants to give me a pelvic massage.

COLONEL   Are you a spiritualist?

WOMAN   I thought he was on his own. I seed 'im and I thought, 'e's a toff.

COLONEL   Ease it off? If you want to ease it off, do it with some of those square-headed German swines.

GERMAN   (*Voice off*.) I heard zat! Englander — take zat!

Enter crowd of German tourists in lederhosen. One of them throttles Van Gogh.

VAN GOGH   (*Choking*.) I am not—

COLONEL   It wasn't him, I said it! We beat you before and we'll beat you again!

German rushes Colonel out. Rembrandt and Van Gogh are quietly drinking their water, as a fight starts out of sight. The fight should be exaggerated in sound. Numerous fist blows. Breaking glasses. Smashing of furniture. A juke box starts to play hard rock. At intervals what appears to be the Colonel (a dummy) hurtles past the Pakistanis. The dummy should be stiff enough so the body remains rigid. Each time the Colonel is hurled across, he looks more battered. Both opponents must keep up threatening dialogue and shouts of pain.

VAN GOGH   (*As Colonel hurtles across, screaming*.) He is going to feel this in the morning.

The Germans start to sing 'Deutschland uber Alles'.

VAN GOGH   Is he losing?

REMBRANDT   Only teeth. (*Regretfully*.) Bapu, I don't think we should let the Germans do this to one of us.

VAN GOGH   They are not doing it to one of us, they are doing it to one of *him*.

Scene 7 *Outside the pub. The door splinters and the Colonel is hurled through. He is a mass of rags. Eyes blackened, he stands up, groaning. From inside the pub comes the sound of Germans singing 'Deutschland uber Alles'.*

COLONEL (*Shouts.*) Had enough, you kraut swines? (*Sings 'God save our gracious Queen...'*)

Police car rushes up, siren going. Policemen descend on Colonel, beat him, bundle him into the boot of the police car, and race off. All this is done to the voices of the Germans singing 'Deutschland uber Alles'. From the car boot, the Colonel continues to sing 'God Save the Queen'.

❁

Scene 8 *Interior of London bus, downstairs. The passengers on the bus are: a well-dressed Chinese couple (male and female), who converse in Chinese; two Hassidic Jewish rabbis, who talk in Hebrew; two well-dressed Hindus in suits, chatting in Hindi, two Ghananian males in native costume, conversing in Ghanaian. Van Gogh and Rembrandt enter and sit on bench seat opposite a drunken Scottish football supporter: middle-aged, unshaven, red-eyed, plaster over his eye. He holds a set of bagpipes that are full of air and groan when the bus accelerates. The Scotsman takes repeated swigs from a whisky bottle, which is partly wrapped in brown paper as a concession to respectability. He keeps swearing, under his breath in a raw Scots accent. Next to him sits a middle-aged man, wearing a large trilby pulled down over his face, and a long mackintosh which reaches nearly to his ankles. His legs are bare. No socks, but white plimsolls. He wears pebble-lens glasses and has staring eyes. Every now and then he starts to shake. Van Gogh and Rembrandt are about to eat from one of those 'Finger lickin' good' fried chicken boxes.*

SCOT   (*Barking at them*.) Woof! Woof! Woof! Havin' yer evening Kit-E-Kat? (*Goes into peals of drunken laughter and then barks again*.)

REMBRANDT   He is warning us not to eat them . . .

VAN GOGH   Don't listen. This is very nice Kentucky Fried Colonel.

SCOT   (*Barks and laughs hysterically. Leans against the bagpipes and they wail and groan*.) Shhhhhhh! This morning that was waggin' its tail in Battersea Dogs' Home!

Tall Jamaican bus conductor comes down.

CONDUCTOR   (*Heavy Jamaican accent*.) Ol' de farz plez, farz plez, ol' de farz plez.

REMBRANDT   Pardon?

CONDUCTOR   I'z sayin'. Can I hev de farz plez.

REMBRANDT   Can you say it slower?

CONDUCTOR   (*Aside*.) Dey mus' be Irish. (*To them*.) Ah said, Farz pleeezzz. Can I have de farz pleeezzz.

VAN GOGH   Farzplez? I haven't any farzplez!

REMBRANDT   (*To Scotsman*.) Please can you tell us what this foreigner is saying?

SCOT   (*Speaks Scottish gibberish*.) Ayeee. Wail, yer see, wan ye're doon heer, ye've car ye eran in a stank and ther's naw ba'blardy Sassenachs . . .

VAN GOGH   (*To conductor*.) What is he saying?

CONDUCTOR   I don't know wot *he* am sayin' but *Ah* am sayin', Farz plez.

At this stage a girl with massive boobs and a very low-cut, skin-tight black top on goes past with a large dog which gobbles Van Gogh's takeaway fried chicken — then dies.

GIRL   (*Screams*.) You've killed my Sambo!

Scene 9 *The front room of No. 7, Piles Road: midnight. Paddy is in his pyjamas and slippers. Newspaper on lap, cup of tea balanced on edge of armchair. Nefertiti sits near him, knitting. Her hair is in curlers with a scarf over the top. Bluey is drinking a tube of Foster's. Van Gogh and Rembrandt are also in their pyjamas, and, with their trilby hats on, are sitting watching TV. Sound of very dreary cello solo. Van Gogh has bandage round his neck.*

REMBRANDT   Don't ever send us to a public house again.

VAN GOGH   What kind of evening is it — a German tries to choke the life out of my neck — and then he fights the English Colonel.

REMBRANDT   And outside they've got the nerve to write 'Drop in at your friendly local' . . .

VAN GOGH   What they should say is: 'Drop in at your friendly local and get the shit knocked out of you'.

BLUEY   You were there on a bad night.

REMBRANDT   You think we didn't know?

VAN GOGH   And the policeman is arresting *us*.

NEFERTITI   What for?

REMBRANDT   He couldn't think of anything and he let us off with a caution and a 50p fine for selling matches.

PADDY   Do you mind keepin' quiet? I'm trying to watch.

BLUEY   How can you watch this bloody rubbish?

PADDY   I'll tell you how. When you're payin' two pounds a week rental you have to watch it all the time otherwise you don't get the value.

They all watch the set for a while, very intently. The boring cello solo continues.

VAN GOGH   Do you have test cards like this in Australia?

BLOODY RUBBISH
TV RENTAL LTD

EPISODE
4

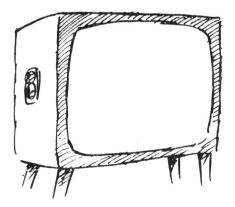

4

Scene 1 *The attic room at No. 7, Piles Road. Van Gogh and Rembrandt are asleep in bed with hats on. They ad lib talking in their sleep. Coming from the next room, the sound of drunken singing, a piano being played, boozy laughter. The Pakistanis sleep on.*

The alarm clock starts to ring. The vibration moves the clock across the bedside cabinet. It moves relentlessly and falls into the po by Rembrandt's bed. There is a loud 'boing' from po. Van Gogh sits bolt upright.

VAN GOGH   *(No teeth in.)* One o'clock! *(He does business, putting teeth in.)*

REMBRANDT   No, no, Bapu. *(He leans out of bed, lifts up the po and looks into it.)* It is exactly seven o'clock.

VAN GOGH   I only heard one.

REMBRANDT   Yes. That was the po striking one. The clock says seven.

VAN GOGH   *(Yawns — teeth fall out.)* Oh, I was dreaming of Mrs Ghandi and fish curry, real hot stuff.

REMBRANDT   Mrs Ghandi is hot stuff?

VAN GOGH   No, Mrs Ghandi is cold stuff — curry is hot stuff — either way I don't give a stuff.

A hatch above Van Gogh's bed opens and the noise of the party comes up. Eight beer cans are thrown through the hatch one after another. Immediately the last can has been thrown the hatch slams shut again. Van Gogh sits up. The hatch opens instantly and a can hits him on the back of head.

VAN GOGH   That bloody Australian! *(Yawns.)* I must do my dawn prayers to the faithful. *(He does an ear-shattering cry.)*

ACCURATE TO THE LAST DROP

REMBRANDT   Wouldn't it be easier to phone them?

Every now and then the hatch opens and beer cans are hurled into room and the hatch door is slammed shut again.

VAN GOGH   The phone is an unclean instrument used by infidels.

REMBRANDT   Why do you say that?

VAN GOGH   Because the Christians are so far away from God they can only get him on the phone, long distance. And when they do get through he's put it on answering service. (*He cups his hand to his mouth.*) Hello. This is Heaven. God is out. Please speak after the tone — pip — pip — pip.

REMBRANDT   I wonder, does he ever get obscene phone calls?

VAN GOGH   Get them? The way their religion is, he makes them! Now. (*He makes a very loud, piercing Moslem call. Hatch opens and a fist with a boxing glove on it smashes him on the jaw and immediately withdraws. The hatch closes again.*) Did you see where my teeth went?

Hatch flies open and Bluey, drunk, pokes his head through. As before, party noise level increases.

BLUEY   Can't you bungs keep quiet, we're trying to have a party in here. (*Plums, raspberry, slams hatch closed.*)

VAN GOGH   That man is a barbarian.

REMBRANDT   What do you expect? He is from *The* Australia.

VAN GOGH   A country run by a man called Fasters.

REMBRANDT   (*Starting to take a pair of shoes out of a plastic bag that has been under his pillow.*) You wait — when we have filled up this country with immigrants — Australia is the next one to get it. (*He is very gleeful.*) Now! Like true Englishman I will prepare myself for a hard day's Social Security. First, remove *Times* newspaper from damp boots. (*He sits down on his bed. As he does so, Van Gogh climbs down from his bunk using Rembrandt as the ladder and tumbles to the ground.*)

HEAVY HEAVENLY BREATHING...

THIS IS A REAL PUNCH NOT A RECORDING

VAN GOGH   Where is ladder?

REMBRANDT   Mr O'Brien is using it to clean the windows.

VAN GOGH   Clean windows with a ladder? I use a cloth.

REMBRANDT   Ah, but he is Irish.

VAN GOGH   He can't be. If he was Irish he would have sent the windows to the laundry.

Rembrandt is removing his pyjama trousers to reveal a pair of very trendy shorts with a message on them: 'I gave at the office.' Van Gogh goes to the window and raises bottom half. He starts to call out in the fashion of a muezzin. Immediately he gets a bucket of water straight in the face. There is laughter from outside the window, then Paddy O'Brien appears.

PADDY   Oh God...I'm sorry about that. (*He starts to mop Van Gogh's face and squeeze it out, then falls out of view. Here is a fading scream, followed by distant crashing glass, howl of tom-cat.*)

VAN GOGH   (*Looking out window.*) My God, he's flattened the cat!

REMBRANDT   He only had the operation yesterday!

The window crashes down on Van Gogh's neck. He yells and shouts. Rembrandt now has his trousers round his ankles. He hobbles across to help Van Gogh. As he is trying to pull him out, Nefertiti comes in carrying fresh sheets for the bed.

NEFERTITI   Here, here, stop that! We're not having anything like that in this house.

REMBRANDT   We've never had anything like this in any house. (*He is very distressed. He pulls up his trousers.*) My father was peeping out of the window.

NEFERTITI   In this country we don't do it out the window!

Suddenly there's a clap of thunder. Van Gogh yells. There is a blue flash of lightning around his head; this creates an instant great pall of blue smoke outside the window.

REMBRANDT   My God, he has been struck by lightning!

Van Gogh extricates himself. As he turns into the room we see that his hat is a charred, smouldering ruin. His head is smoking and his neck is at a very acute angle.

NEFERTITI   Don't worry, Mr Rembrandt, lightning never strikes twice in the same place.

Van Gogh smiles and faints.

✦

Scene 2   *The front room at No. 7, Piles Road. Nefertiti is topping up a half-full bottle of milk with water. The entire household is at the table, with the exception of Van Gogh, Rembrandt and Paddy.*

NEFERTITI   (*More or less to herself.*) What's good enough for the cat is good enough for the kaffirs.

Paddy enters. He has sticking plaster on his nose and chin, a large bruise on his forehead, a bandage on his hand. His clothes are dirty.

PADDY   That's the last time I clean those windows.

NEFERTITI   As I recall, it's also the *first* time.

PADDY   (*Now at the table, picking up newspaper.*) Now, what crap have we got today?

NEFERTITI   You've got the sausage. (*She drops the sausage on to the plate. It lands with a loud clang.*)

PADDY   Anybody got a saw?

BLUEY   Yes, I got a saw — a sore bum! (*Goes into terrible hyena-like laughter.*) Heah—heah—heah— Now you see, in Australia they'd laugh at that!

PADDY   Oh, I'm sure they'd laugh at that.

There is an array of sauce bottles on the table, including one that is clearly labelled 'Filth'. This is the one that Paddy picks up. He sprays it liberally all over the sausage.

PADDY   (*Barks.*) Down boy! (*He bangs the sausage on the plate. It bounces.*) If you saw a thing like that in the desert, what would you do?

RICHARD   He'd worship it.

YAMANI   If *you* found it you'd put it in your wife's name.

RICHARD   I refuse to have any truck with Arabs. Not that they've got any trucks — they left 'em all behind in the Six-Day War.

PADDY   (*Reads from label.*) Genuine grade one Japanese Ahso Brown Sauce made under licence in Hong Kong.

BLUEY   It must be a bloody dog licence. Heah—heah—heah. Now you see, in Australia they'd all laugh at that.

PADDY   Ingredients: ninety-nine per cent pure simulated cellulose-type tomato juice. Keep away from naked flame.

ERIC FUNG   What's the one per cent, then?

PADDY   Real artificial colouring.

YAMANI   I'll be glad when I've left this infidel land — back to Arabia!

RICHARD   We'll *all* be glad.

YAMANI   Have you ever spent a night in the desert under the stars?

BLUEY   Yes.

YAMANI   Wasn't it romantic?

BLUEY   It was bloody terrible.

YAMANI   Why?

AEROSOL FILTH

BLUEY   Rommel was knocking the crap out of us, that's why.

There is a moan off, and then Van Gogh and Rembrandt enter. Van Gogh is holding his neck to one side.

PADDY   Here he comes, the Englebert Humperdinck of the Ganges, wearing one of the top ten loincloths which has now slipped to number three.

VAN GOGH   Don't laugh. I think I've broken my dashed neck

PADDY   Look, *I* fell off the ladder. If anyone's entitled to a broken neck, it's me.

NEFERTITI   Right. If anybody's entitled to a broken neck, it's him.

Cuckoo clock on wall goes 'Cuckoo, Cuckoo'.

PADDY   (*Shouting at clock.*) Ah, shut yer mouth! (*He takes sausage and hurls it at the clock. The sausage misses the clock and crashes through the wall.*) Did you see that? It went straight through the wall.

VAN GOGH   It was supposed to go through you.

PADDY   What can you do with them? They're not like us English.

There's complete silence while the various nationalities at the table look round at each other.

VAN GOGH   Oh? And which of us English are we not like?

PADDY   You're not like *any* of us English.

VAN GOGH   It's only by the colour you can tell. Close your eyes. Guess who's talking.

Paddy puts hands over his eyes.

VAN GOGH   Ready? Hello, old toff. By jove, there goes the Derby winner now. Isn't that the Chelsea Flower show sinking off Brighton? Jolly good. Can I borrow a cup of sugar? You swine! God save our Queen. Now — who spoke?

PADDY   You?

VAN GOGH   You looked. Ooohh! (*He grabs his neck*.) Pain in the neck!

PADDY   Right!

REMBRANDT   Do you know where my father can get his neck repaired?

BLUEY   Calcutta!

REMBRANDT   Shut up, silly — silly — *convict*!

PADDY   The best man is Dr Brett. He has a practice in Harley Street.

VAN GOGH   If he still has to practise, I'm not going to him. (*He yells as his neck hurts*.)

REMBRANDT   Is medicine still free in our country?

PADDY   No, but illness is!

RICHARD   Get away. Look what I got yesterday. (*Reads from small list*.) Two hundred and fifty Tuinal, two bottles syrup of figs, two rolls cotton wool, NHS— (*he produces these things*).

PADDY   Good God . . . if you take the first you'll be asleep in twenty minutes. That's alright. *But*, if you take the first and the second as well, then something's going to happen in the middle of the night, and you won't be awake to know about it and when you *do* wake up you'll wish to God you were still asleep.

BLUEY   (*Throws down newspaper*.) This country! There's more bloody medicine stashed away in cupboards, under beds, in the back of garages, than they have in the bloody hospitals. You know where the National Health Service shop for their medicines? Portobello Road Market! Last Saturday a woman collapsed with appendicitis in front of a surgical stall — the barrow boy had so much gear he operated himself. And when she came round he sold her a Georgian tea service.

RICHARD   Alright, so I get my medicine *before* I'm struck down. In the words of Baden-Powell — be prepared. What kept the Israelites alive in the desert?

YAMANI   Food parcels from Tesco's.

RICHARD   Tesco's! — It was *Moses*.

VAN GOGH   They had food parcels from *Moses*?

Richard shuts Van Gogh up with a few words of Hebrew invective.

VAN GOGH   (*In Urdu.*) Chupperow them milo. Suer. Up your synagogue!

REMBRANDT   NHS is very good. There is no racial discrimination, is there, on the National Health?

PADDY   Oh no, there's one thing you can't get on the National Health and that's racial discrimination.

REMBRANDT   I mean, you don't have to be white?

PADDY   No, colour makes no difference. Unless you've got jaundice. Then you have to be yellow.

VAN GOGH   So then the Chinkiepoo here, he is being treated for jaundice.

ERIC FUNG   Stuff it! Chinkiepoo. Before this lot came in, *I* used to be a *London cockney*. Now I'm a Chinkiepoo. I'll 'ave to get an eye job done. Trouble is, it costs two hundred quid. I've only got a 'undred.

PADDY   Well, have one done and wear a black patch over the other.

☼

Scene 3   *A shabby doctor's waiting-room. Sound of flies buzzing. There are World War Two posters — very faded. All the wallpaper's coming off the walls, there are newspapers on the floor. There are four or five kitchen chairs with bits of the backs missing, a couch which has springs sticking out and which has been patched up with sticky tape. A naked light bulb hangs down. There are two Nigerian women in national costume, a Sikh, a one-legged Scotsman in a kilt with his leg in plaster, a cockney woman with a midget with a po wedged firmly on his head. There is a very dark African in an ankle-length white coat. There is also a grey-faced man with a hankie to his face who just coughs all the time. Van Gogh and Rembrandt enter.*

REMBRANDT   Pardon me, is this where the illness is?

COCKNEY WOMAN   Well, there wasn't.

VAN GOGH   Which one of you is Dr Stonehouse?

COCKNEY WOMAN   (*Shouts.*) They're in there — they're both in there! You 'ave to waitee 'ere, darlin'.

Van Gogh sits next to her.

MIDGET   (*With po on head.*) I'm getting 'ungry, Mum.

COCKNEY WOMAN   (*Shouts.*) Not long now, darlin'. (*To Van Gogh.*) He fell out of bed in the night, you know.

VAN GOGH   No, I didn't know...

COCKNEY WOMAN   Head first. We was up all night with 'im. We 'ad to go next door and use theirs...we're squatters, you know.

VAN GOGH   You'd have to squat with one of those. (*Sound of neck rattle and he groans.*)

COCKNEY WOMAN   (*To Rembrandt.*) 'Ere, have you come over for wigs and teeth?

VAN GOGH   No, we have come over for a broken neck.

The dreadful coughing which has been going on in the backgorund now breaks into a fierce spasm.

COCKNEY WOMAN   Don't you bring that up in 'ere, will you?

There's a terrible scream from inside the doctor's surgery and then the sound of a cash register. The door to the surgery opens and two people carry out a gas inspector on a stretcher.

COCKNEY WOMAN   Cor, look at this poor geezer!

REMBRANDT   Oh dearie me, madam, what was wrong with him?

COCKNEY WOMAN   I dunno. He only came in to read the gas meter.

VAN GOGH   I've just read *One Flew over the Cuckoo's Nest*

Enter a very busty nurse with tight white apron.

NURSE   (*French accent.*) Mr Mgolo Mgolo? (*Pause.*) All right then...Mrs Wretch...Dr Swine will see you now. (*Turns to Rembrandt.*) Eet weel be your turn for eet next.

At this point nurse drops pencil. She bends down to pick it up, revealing deep cleavage to Rembrandt. When she stands up straight, he takes the pencil from her and throws it to the ground again. She picks it up and he starts to reach for the pencil again. The nurse pulls skittishly away and Rembrandt takes a pencil from his own pocket and throws it on the ground.

From the surgery comes the sound of a po being smashed by a hammer. The pieces fall to the ground and a child screams. In the waiting-room Van Gogh stands up, reacting to these sounds.

Cockney woman and the midget come out from the surgery. The midget has now got a bald head with a white sticking plaster over a lump in the middle.

MIDGET   Oh, my bleedin' head.

COCKNEY WOMAN   Stop moanin' — it's not bleeding. And anyway, the nice doctor said 'e'd get you a wig with a 'ole in the middle, didn't he?

VAN GOGH   How strange — the child looks older than its mother. *That* is the permissive society...you turn your back on children and while you're not looking they grow older than you, die first, and you have to pay for the funeral.

NURSE   You are next. (*Van Gogh and Rembrandt enter the surgery.*) Mr Mgolo Mgolo? (*Pause.*) He should've been here four hours ago. (*She turns to the very black man in the long white coat.*) Excuse me, what's your name?

MAN   (*Cups his hand to his ear, shouts.*) What?

NURSE   (*Shouting.*) What's your name?

MAN   Mgolo Mgolo, and I have been waiting here for four hours.

❖

Scene 4   *The doctor's surgery: a magnificent room in direct contrast to the waiting-room. The doctor is Germanic... But more Himmler than Hitler. He is writing notes.*

NURSE   Mr Van Gogh and Mr Rembrandt.

DOCTOR   Yes. (*Looks up.*) Aarrgh! Gott in Himmel! Schwartzers! (*He reaches into drawer, pulls out two wigs and two sets of teeth and places them on the desk in front of the Pakistanis.*) Here are ze wigs ... und here ze teeth ... now sign here.

VAN GOGH   Wait — there is something else.

DOCTOR   Zere's nothing else I can do for you. You will be zat colour till the day you die. Next, please.

REMBRANDT   He is next, please.

DOCTOR   Vot is it?

VAN GOGH   A pain in the neck.

DOCTOR   You're *all* a pain in ze neck!

VAN GOGH   The window is crashing down on my neck.

DOCTOR   Now, tell me if this hurts. (*Presses Van Gogh's neck.*)

VAN GOGH   (*Screams.*) Yes!

DOCTOR   Exactly vere is der pain?

VAN GOGH   Still in the window. Ha! Ha!

DOCTOR   (*Pressing neck with great force.*) I hate Hindu humour.

Van Gogh screams.

Scene 5 *The street outside doctor's surgery. Van Gogh (his neck in plaster) and Rembrandt issue forth from surgery. They step off the pavement and disappear round corner. A brief pause, then sound of car crash, followed by running footsteps.*

The footsteps approach and Colonel Grope appears. His jacket is ripped down the front and covered in oil. He is wearing a straw boater, the brim of which has been torn from the front and hangs down the back so that it keeps flapping. He holds a pair of upright handlebars with the old-fashioned carbide lamp hanging open. Draped over the handlebars is a Harrods carrier bag.

COLONEL   Bloody fool! Bloody fool! Went straight across a green light. (*Sees crashed car.*) Datsun! I *knew* it would be a bloody foreigner... ruined me Rudge Whitworth. (*Looks into his lamp.*) Oh, the bulb's gone! (*Recognizes make of crashed car.*) Bloody Japanese! Did anybody see that accident?

VAN GOGH   (*From under car.*) Yes... I did.

COLONEL   Good! Where are you, man?

VAN GOGH   Down here.

COLONEL   Where's down here?

VAN GOGH   I don't know, but wherever it is, that's where I am.

Colonel hurriedly bends down. He shouts under car.

COLONEL   Did you see the accident?

VAN GOGH   See it — I *was* it!

COLONEL   Even better! I'll need you as a witness. (*He starts to pull Van Gogh out by the legs.*) Forty-eight years' no-claims bonus on this bike, and now this! (*He sees Van Gogh's face.*) Good God, he's black in the face... asphyxia!

VAN GOGH   (*Moans.*) No! Pakistani.

COLONEL   Good! The best type of accident — bloody foreigners! I'll need you as a witness. (*He brings out a tape recorder.*) Now. (*Retests the set.*) Testing, testing.

Now — in court you will say after me: 'As God is my witness, it was the foreign car-driver's fault.'

Van Gogh very faintly repeats.

COLONEL 'But for the prompt action of a kindly English retired Colonel, who is entirely blameless, I wouldn't be standing in this court today.'

Van Gogh passes out with a groan.

COLONEL No...no...don't go yet! Ah! The kiss of life.

Colonel makes to give kiss of life. He becomes aware of a pair of legs; his eyes travel upwards and he sees the black constable.

CONSTABLE Two men kissing.

COLONEL I'm giving him the kiss of life—

CONSTABLE Oh? You naughty man—

COLONEL I'm innocent, I tell you, listen to this. (*Switches on tape recorder which immediately plays a recording of Jack Hulbert singing 'The Sun has got his Hat on...Hip Hip Hooray'.*)

✺

Scene 6 *A hospital maternity ward. Three of the beds are occupied by pregnant women – one Chinese, two black – and in the fourth bed is Van Gogh with his left leg and left arm in traction. Rembrandt enters with a nurse. His head is bandaged, but he still wears his hat, which is looking a bit tattered. His arm is in a sling.*

REMBRANDT Bapu — what are you doing in a maternity bed?

VAN GOGH I'm not doing anything in it. They bring a bottle round.

REMBRANDT You're not an expectant mother.

VAN GOGH I'm not even an expectant father. It is because of overcrowding. What happened to you?

REMBRANDT   I don't know. I've been unconscious for the last two days.

VAN GOGH   What ward are you in?

REMBRANDT   Florence Nightingale bronchitis ward.

VAN GOGH   You had bronchitis?

REMBRANDT   No, but I've got it now.

At the foot appear Paddy, Nefertiti, Richard with flowers, etc.

NEFERTITI   You wouldn't believe me...I told you he was in here.

VAN GOGH   It was an accident. Look at me. (*Moans.*) I wish I had never left Calcutta.

RICHARD   Easy, easy. (*Gets out calculator.*) In a private ward this would cost you four hundred nicker.

Eric Fung rushes in with a cake box.

ERIC FUNG   Sorry I'm late — the rush hour —

NEFERTITI   Your son told us it was your sixty-second birthday, Mr Van Gogh.

VAN GOGH   He must have counted the wrinkles on it.

Nefertiti opens the cake box, lifts out cake.

NEFERTITI   I've made it the way you like it — curried.

All sing 'Happy Birthday'. The others join in and as they do so a black nurse enters with a white baby. She places the baby in the cradle of Van Gogh's arm.

NURSE   It am time to feed de baby, Mrs Goldstein.

VAN GOGH   Mrs Goldstein?

EPISODE
5

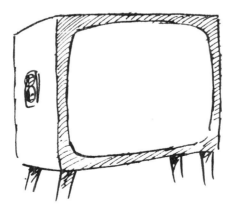

Scene 1 *Early Sunday morning in Soho. A white Rolls Royce is parked outside a prostitute's pad, advertised by a card with the words 'Miss Whiplash — pelvic massage'. An old boy of ninety comes out. He steps on a drunk, asleep in the alleyway. The tart follows the old boy out.*

TART   Same time next Sunday, your Lordship?

LORD   Oh, yes, next time with custard. (*He is helped into car by chauffeur and, as they drive off*) Woburn . . .

Van Gogh has been watching all this. As the Rolls drives off he walks forward. The tart turns to go in and notices him.

TART   Looking for a good time, sailor?

VAN GOGH   No, I know the time, thank you.

Van Gogh walks on. He stumbles over the drunk, who retches. This is the cue for the lid of a large-sized restaurant dustbin to push up, revealing a pair of eyes.

MALE VOICE   (*From dustbin.*) Want a nice time with a dwarf, sailor?

VAN GOGH   Four-thirty.

FEMALE VOICE   (*From dustbin.*) What did he say?

MALE VOICE   Four-thirty.

FEMALE VOICE   Miserable bastard. 'Ere, put the cat out.

Cat is thrown out of dustbin. Van Gogh walks on. He is accosted by a drunk coming down the street.

DRUNK   My mother...my mother was a lovely woman.

VAN GOGH   Thank you.

DRUNK   Don't thank me...things could go wrong for you...I suppose you think that's bloody funny? Well, watch it — I'm an Aries.

He begins to shake Van Gogh. A policeman arrives.

CONSTABLE   Excuse me, sir, is this Asian immigrant annoying you?

DRUNK   My mother—

CONSTABLE   I see, he's after your mother, is he?

The drunk now embraces the policeman.

DRUNK   Mother — mother — you became a policeman.

CONSTABLE   Get 'im off me! Get 'im off! Stop that — stop—

The drunk starts to kiss policeman. At that moment a photographer's flash bulb explodes. Policeman jumps.

CONSTABLE   'Ere, give me that camera, you — (*He exits, shouting.*) Give me that bleedin' camera.

The drunk turns back to Van Gogh and drops a cigarette. He bends down to pick it up but is beaten to it by a hand that comes out of a manhole cover. Van Gogh walks on.

Scene 2   *Outside No. 7, Piles Road. A Salvation Army band is walking up the road. The Major leading them has a book.*

MAJOR   (*Consulting his book.*) Number 7, Piles Road...Piles Road. Occupants Catholic. Right, double loud!

The band plays a very loud, beaty version of 'Onward, Christian Soldiers'.

Scene 3 *Paddy's bedroom inside No. 7, Piles Road. Paddy is fast asleep as the sound of the band blasts into the room. His eyes open.*

PADDY Proddys!

✿

Scene 4 *Outside No. 7, Piles Road. An upstairs window is pushed up. A bucket of water is poured over the band. With the aid of a concealed hose pipe, a jet of water shoots straight out of the euphonium, back up into Paddy's face.*

✿

Scene 5 *The attic room at No. 7, Piles Road. Rembrandt is asleep. The door opens and Van Gogh tiptoes in, carrying newspapers. Rembrandt wakes.*

REMBRANDT Are you awake, Bapu?

VAN GOGH Of course — you don't think I sleep standing up?

REMBRANDT What are you doing up so early?

VAN GOGH I am beating the rush hour. You know, those long queues at the Social Security. Well — none.

REMBRANDT Today is Sunday.

VAN GOGH Of course, the English have it off on weekends.

REMBRANDT Wrong, they have the weekend off.

VAN GOGH Have you read the Sunday papers?

REMBRANDT No.

VAN GOGH Believe me — the English are having it off this weekend. Why is it that all the ladies in Soho think I'm in the Navy?

REMBRANDT   Hello, sailor?

VAN GOGH   Yes. Sometimes — 'Hello Cheeky, want to give your trousers a rest?' I was walking by a shop — and a poof is kissing me!

REMBRANDT   You ran away?

VAN GOGH   Oh yes — I had to. I was starting to enjoy it.

Hatch in wall opens. Bluey Notts looks through.

BLUEY   Will you bloody bungs shut up? This is a Christian Sunday — the bloody Sabbath!

VAN GOGH   What is the time, please?

BLUEY   I'll give yer the time — in Sydney it's one o'clock — in Melbourne it's 4.20—

VAN GOGH   But in Brixton?

BLUEY   In Brixton it's bloody awful!

Van Gogh reads paper. There is a knock at the door.

VAN GOGH   Who is it?

NEFERTITI   It's me — Nefertiti. Are you decent?

REMBRANDT   No — just respectable.

Nefertiti comes in wearing the scantiest of clothing: black shortie nightie with jet black pants, and lurid bedroom slippers. She is carrying a bottle of milk.

VAN GOGH   Why did you ask if we were decent? We should be asking you. If a woman dressed like that in Bangladesh, do you know what would happen to her?

NEFERTITI   No.

VAN GOGH   Thank God for that.

NEFERTITI   I've only come to ask you, have you heard anybody banging away upstairs?

REMBRANDT   Not yet, but thanks for the tip.

NEFERTITI   We got some men upstairs, they're converting the loft.

The bottom drawer of a very wide chest of drawers is pushed open from behind. There is a crazed, doubled-up figure inside. He is black and wears pyjamas with a blanket over him.

MAN IN DRAWER   I don't know how you can charge me fifteen pounds a week for dis!

NEFERTITI   (*Pushing the drawer back in.*) You wanted equality with the whites — now you've got it, you're complaining. You see, we are desperately trying to help people who have no place to stay.

She taps on the cupboard and puts the milk down. As she continues talking the cupboard door opens slightly and a hand takes the bottle and replaces it with an empty one with a note in it. There is the sound of singing from inside the cupboard. Almost immediately the cupboard door opens and a dwarf walks out wearing pyjamas, dressing-gown and army boots. He sings 'If I Ruled the World . . .'

NEFERTITI   Good morning, Garth.

DWARF   Good morning, Nefertiti. I'm just going to have a bath.

VAN GOGH   You'd better take a lifebelt. Mrs Nefertiti, I find your dress very, very disturbing.

REMBRANDT   (*Confidentially.*) Look, I want to tell you something about my old man.

NEFERTITI   I don't want to hear anything about your old man. I had enough trouble with mine. But he was a wonderful husband! Here's a picture of him. (*She leans forward to show Rembrandt a picture that is in a locket round her neck.*) He had a very good position.

REMBRANDT   He's still in a good position.

Scene 6 *The front room at No. 7, Piles Road. The entire household except for Bluey is at the table.*

NEFERTITI (*Putting tins out on the table*.) I'm sorry about all this cold stuff, they've cut off the gas.

She puts a blue plate with what looks suspiciously like Kit-E-Kat on it down on the table near Rembrandt.

PADDY Never mind. Get it down you, that'll soon warm it up!

VAN GOGH (*Reading from label on tin*.) Irish stew — made in Paraguay. Must be eaten before 4th June 1937. Why do we have to eat it before then?

PADDY Because dat's your last chance.

Rembrandt starts to eat the stuff from the blue plate.

PADDY (*He has taken the tin from Van Gogh*.) Anyways, Paraguayans don't know how to make Irish stew. And I should know.

VAN GOGH Why?

PADDY Why? I'm Irish, and *we* don't know how to make Irish stew.

VAN GOGH (*Reads label*.) Look what you can win with these wrappers. (*He passes tin to Rembrandt*.)

REMBRANDT Double-bunk family-sized glass two-tone glitter gold Riviera Caravan. Wall-to-wall floor, chrome-type tap complete with extra washer.

RICHARD How many wrappers do you need?

REMBRANDT Two hundred thousand.

PADDY It's a rip-off.

VAN GOGH Oh yes, you have to rip them off.

PADDY How you gonna eat two hundred thousand Irish stews before June?

WE ONLY NEED 199,999 MORE WRAPPERS

RICHARD   No, no, no. Listen. If you want to win that caravan, what you do is form an eating club. You get two hundred thousand hungry buggers (*takes out pocket calculator and starts doing sums*) all eating the stuff for ten days and you've done it!

VAN GOGH   How can you stuff two hundred thousand people in a double-bunk caravan?

PADDY   Youse take turns.

RICHARD   You don't. You put all the names into a hat. Then you draw one out and he wins. Taa-raa!

REMBRANDT   What about the other 199,999?

RICHARD   Oh, sod them.

VAN GOGH   Here you are, eating two hundred thousand Irish stews for a caravan. In my country millions are starving.

PADDY   It's your own fault, there's too many of you.

VAN GOGH   What you mean, there's too many of me? There's only one of me.

PADDY   No, *population*. It's all that curry you eat, it acts as an aphrodisiac. It filters through into your loin-cloth.

VAN GOGH   I see, it reaches the parts of the system that other aphrodisiacs cannot reach!

PADDY   You must admit, in India they're always at it.

VAN GOGH   At what?

PADDY   The other.

VAN GOGH   What other?

PADDY   The old dum di di dum dum (*on the last two he makes gesture with his arm*) dum dum.

VAN GOGH   Dum dum? What is he talking about? Dum?

RICHARD   He's saying that in India, they're banging away day and night.

VAN GOGH   Like the Irish workmen in the loft.

Nefertiti arrives at the table with a couple of plates of food.

NEFERTITI   Here, who ate the stuff on the blue plate?

REMBRANDT   I did.

NEFERTITI   It was the cat's.

REMBRANDT   Oh my God! (*Clutches at his throat*.)

NEFERTITI   Don't worry. It's perfectly good food.

Rembrandt relaxes. Bluey enters the room.

BLUEY   'Ere, your pussy cat's dead.

REMBRANDT   Ahhhhhh...

VAN GOGH   Quick, someone, call a doctor.

REMBRANDT   (*Continuing*.) Ahhhhhh...miaow. Miaow.

VAN GOGH   Never mind a doctor, call a vet.

REMBRANDT   Miaow...miaow.

❀

Scene 7   *The front room: a little later. The room is littered with the lurid Sunday papers. The TV is on. The programme is a repeat of the summer Test Matches highlights. Luigi is watching. Van Gogh and Rembrandt are doing something at the table. Bluey is drinking lager. Nefertiti is ironing a pair of trousers. Richard is reading an Israeli newspaper.*

REMBRANDT   What language paper is that?

RICHARD   It's Hebrew. Can't you read? (*Reads from paper*.) It's the *Sinai Sun*.

YAMANI   Printed in Cairo.

RICHARD   That's because it's cheaper. Gypos will work for next to nothing.

VAN GOGH   Talking of next to nothing, could I have some dinner on this plate?

NEFERTITI   There *is* something on it.

VAN GOGH   Oh, I thought it was a stain.

NEFERTITI   What are you insinuating? Kaffir!

VAN GOGH   Nothing, nothing. It's a beautifully-cooked stain. Yum, yum, yum. Could I have a second helping of stain, please?

BLUEY   (*Watching the television*.) Beaut! Beaut!

PADDY   What's that?

BLUEY   It's great! They're repeating all the Test Matches.

PADDY   Are Australia batting?

BLUEY   Yes.

PADDY   I'd better not bend down to pick up dat spoon or they'll be out by the time I get up again.

BLUEY   See Botham! He is bowling with two short legs and a long on.

VAN GOGH   They shouldn't let a cripple like that play.

Nefertiti comes across the room with the trousers. She hands them to Van Gogh who stands up, revealing that he's wearing long underpants.

PADDY   Luigi, youse is coloured. When youse go to a Test Match, say England's playing the West Indies, who do you support?

LUIGI   I support England.

PADDY   Do you sit with the nig-nogs or with the colonels in their blazers?

LUIGI   Well...er, I must admit I feel more comfortable sitting among the niggers.

PADDY   You're lying. You hide yourself in the nig-nogs because you know that if they saw you sitting with whites you'd be found in Brixton with a spear up your back.

BLUEY   That's if they didn't eat 'im first. (*Terrible hyena laugh.*)

REMBRANDT   And don't forget if it wasn't for Pakistanis, you wouldn't have any county cricket teams.

PADDY   If they're not opening grocery shops they're opening the batting.

VAN GOGH   And jolly good hit cricketers they are. Whack, whack, whack they go, toodle pip, another boundary. He'll never stop it.

BLUEY   When Australia send a cricket team here you don't find four Pakistanis, two bungs, a Chinaman—

NEFERTITI   (*Interrupting.*) Or a South African captain. Don't forget it was Tony Greig who led the British cricket team—

PADDY   (*Interrupting.*) To four successive defeats!

LUIGI   What are you talking about! What do the Irish know about cricket?

PADDY   England were skiddled out by the West Indians, that's what the Irish know.

RICHARD   (*Laughing hugely at his own wit.*) This is the Irish 'no'! (*He nods his head affirmatively.*)

PADDY   Very funny. There he is — Israel's ambassador of comedy — kills ninety-nine per cent of all known jokes.

BLUEY   (*Watching TV set.*) Look at that! My old man died from a better stroke.

LUIGI   Listen, we taught you to play the game.

BLUEY   Let me tell you, midnight, when we were learning to play, your lot were still working out how to climb down the trees.

PADDY   And when they saw *your* lot, they started climbing back up them again.

BLUEY   That's right. And they met *your* lot coming down. (*Laughs like mad.*)

LUIGI   Would you listen to him! A hundred years ago his lot were breaking rocks, chained to a tree in Paramatta.

BLUEY   (*Leaning over.*) Listen, clever dick —

RICHARD   He's certainly got one of those.

BLUEY   I got more right to be in this country than the whole bloody lot of you. (*He pauses — grins hugely.*) I come from old English farming stock.

PADDY   You sure you weren't laughing stock?

REMBRANDT   All finished! Good! In the absence of getting some sleep this afternoon, my father and I are going to see Hyde Park on the tube.

VAN GOGH   Tell me, are all the flowers out in the Park?

PADDY   Oh yeah...The lads ripped 'em out months ago.

BLUEY   But you might find a few pommie pansies in Kensington Gardens.

REMBRANDT   (*Looking in GLC brochure.*) We are going to Speaker's Corner. Not far from where stood the Tyburn Gallows where they hanged the Martyrs!

PADDY   (*Beams.*) They were trade unionists asking for more money.

VAN GOGH   Oh, jolly good. They'll be hanging hundreds of them today.

NEFERTITI   (*Opening an envelope.*) We got the final demand for the water rates — £28.12p.

PADDY   My God — it's cheaper to wash in Guinness.

REMBRANDT   We must hurry, Bapu, to be in the bandstand at 3.30 o'clock.

Very slowly Bluey starts to sing, drunkenly.

BLUEY   I'm going back to Yarra Wonga... In Yarra Winga I'll linger longer.

As he sings, one by one the people get up and leave the room. Alone, he finishes the song. He starts to sing 'Waltzing Matilda'. The door behind him opens; Paddy enters and beats Bluey on head. He falls face down onto table. Paddy exits.

✿

Scene 8   Hyde Park Corner. A speaker is declaiming. It is Colonel Grope. He is wearing tweed plus-fours, Royal Engineers tie, and his medals. Van Gogh and Rembrandt, eating candy floss, are standing in a crowd that is composed entirely of foreigners and is being patrolled by a policeman.

COLONEL   My dear fellow-countrymen... Englishmen.

VAN GOGH   He means us.

COLONEL   It is the blackamoor and the brownamoor who are ruining this corner of a foreign field that is forever England.

JAMAICAN   Shut up!

COLONEL   Shut up? Would any of you want your daughter to marry a black man?

JAMAICAN   Oh yes, man. We am very choosy in Brixton.

COLONEL   (*Ignoring this.*) And another political danger — Chinese food. That's what's giving the country all this stomach trouble. Where there's a Chinkiepoo restaurant there's a take-away disease!

JAMAICAN   Crap!

COLONEL   It is crap! Shut up! It's time we English stood together. Help me put this tune in the charts. (*Sings.*) God save our gracious white Queen. (*Goes round with a collection box.*)

REMBRANDT   You collecting for the Queen?

COLONEL   Yes, and the National White Front Union of Wimbledon.

VAN GOGH   You're not *white*. *You're* red!

COLONEL   Me, a Red! One more word out of you and I'll run you out of England to Southall!

JAMAICAN   No! One more word out of you and de buses won't be runnin' tonight.

POLICEMAN   Come along now, please, the show is over. Same time tomorrow.

Everybody except Rembrandt and Van Gogh moves off. The Colonel holds out collection box.

COLONEL   Help save England from the Jews.

REMBRANDT   (*Proffers a ten-pound note.*) Do you have any change?

COLONEL   Ten pounds! (*He puts ten-pound note in his pocket.*) No! (*He greedily eyes all the money in Rembrandt's wallet. It's thick with Social Security payments.*) Is that all money in there? (*He taps wallet.*)

VAN GOGH   Yes. We are saving up to buy something.

COLONEL   Don't tell me — the Hilton Hotel. How much do you have altogether?

REMBRANDT   In the region of a hundred and twenty-five pounds.

COLONEL   I've never lived in that region. Look, I don't say this to everybody: I am a financial wizard!

Policeman coughs to attract Colonel's attention.

COLONEL   Just a minute. (*He hands policeman a bribe.*)

REMBRANDT   He is giving him a cough sweet.

COLONEL   (*Returns.*) No, these vast sums of money you are carrying — even as you stand, the pound is devaluing, getting less.

VAN GOGH   Oh no. We count it every half hour and it always comes to the same amount.

COLONEL That's no good. You want to invest in something that's going to increase in value and to give you something for your old age.

VAN GOGH I've already got something for my old age.

COLONEL What?

VAN GOGH Rheumatism.

COLONEL That's not good enough. Now, let me show you ... (*He leads them off.*)

The Jamaican takes over the speaker's stand.

JAMAICAN What am ruinin' de country am all dese honkies ...

❂

Scene 9 *The Colonel, Van Gogh and Rembrandt are standing beside the Albert Memorial.*

COLONEL (*Slapping a 'sold' label on it.*) There — at twenty pounds, a bargain, and a *must* for the garden ... And I'll have it sent round in a van in the morning, Number 7, Piles Road, is it?

EPISODE
6

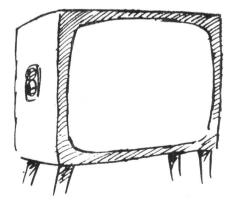

6

Scene 1 *The attic room, No. 7, Piles Road. Rain is dripping from the ceiling into a bucket. The cupboard door opens and the dwarf emerges. He puts down an empty milk bottle, and waves goodbye to his wife in the cupboard.*

DWARF (*Exiting.*) Bye-bye, dear . . . don't forget the prunes. (*He slams door. The light fitting falls from ceiling.*)

VAN GOGH (*Waking up, no teeth in.*) It is time to get up. (*Puts teeth in — clacking noise. He climbs down the ladder.*)

REMBRANDT You're not getting up — you are getting down. What do we have to get up for? We are unemployed.

VAN GOGH That is right. It is time for us to get up to be *ready* for our unemployment, like the other three million.

REMBRANDT If I know the British, those three million are still in bed trying to make it four million.

VAN GOGH Even though we have no work to do, it is good to get up early to be in time to do it. (*Starts wailing Moslem prayers. He goes to the door, on which is pinned a piece of paper with writings from the Koran, and adopts a praying position.*)

Hammering starts on the wall. Throughout the hammering Van Gogh goes on praying.

PADDY (*Off.*) Will youse pull de chain out dere!

Van Gogh continues to pray. Increased hammering on the wall.

PADDY (*Off.*) Can youse hear me in dere?

IN CASE OF
FIRE RECITE

The door bursts open and Van Gogh's head goes through the lower panel. Paddy's head appears through the half-open door. He wears ill-fitting blue serge trousers — which he is holding up — a shirt and braces, and he is clutching a newspaper.

PADDY   (*To Rembrandt.*) Where's your father?

VAN GOGH   I'm outside, here in the hall.

Paddy comes in and disengages the door from Van Gogh's head.

VAN GOGH   I was at my morning devotions.

PADDY   And I was at mine! Listen, youse two. You only got dis Winston Churchill Memorial Suite cheap *provided* you pulls de chain in here when anybody bangs on de kazi wall.

REMBRANDT   Please let me explain. My father was praying towards Mecca.

PADDY   (*Pointing over shoulder.*) Mecca? That's Brixton.

VAN GOGH   Ooooh — what a terrible thing! I was praying to end the drought in Bangladesh and all the time I was praying to Brixton.

PADDY   So *that's* why we're getting all this bloody rain. (*Throws his newspaper down. Sniffs.*) Ah! Eggs and bacon. (*Exits.*)

REMBRANDT   Wait till he finds it's coming from next door.

VAN GOGH   If I know him he's *going* next door.

Van Gogh and Rembrandt are now taking off their pyjamas. Rembrandt has switched on the transistor radio. There is non-stop gunge coming from it.)

NEFERTITI   (*From below.*) Come and get it before it gets cold.

VAN GOGH   How can All Bran get cold?

Scene 2 *The front room. The table is laid for breakfast. There is a complete packet advertising 'Famous Footballer Series. In this packet — a plastic Sir Alf Ramsey.' There are two plastic footballers already on the table. Eric Lee Fung, obviously looking for Sir Alf, is emptying the packet on to his plate. He keeps emptying it until eventually the whole packet overflows his plate. He tries to put the cornflakes back in the packet.*

ERIC   That's a swizz — there ain't no Alf Ramsey in 'ere.

LUIGI   (*Jumping up and spitting all his cornflakes out.*) I think I've swallowed him — were 'e in your packet? (*He indicates another cornflake packet on the table.*)

ERIC   No, that was George Best. (*He stands up six plastic footballers.*) What a choker — all I needed was Sir Alf for the set.

VAN GOGH   Pardon me, is this Alf Ramsey I'm scraping on my bread? (*Eric takes the plastic figure and cleans it in Van Gogh's tea.*)

PADDY   What terrible manners! You don't dip a jam-covered Sir Alf in some poor bloody wog's tea.

REMBRANDT   (*Angry.*) Objection, we are not *wogs*, we are sun-tanned gentlemen. And we are British Shitizens! We are subjects of the Queen, Prince Philip and Social Security to the value of £17.50 per week. I am protected by this passport! (*He produces passport.*)

PADDY   (*Snatches passport.*) Let's see dat! This passport picture — it's Tommy Cooper!

VAN GOGH   Yes — I stuck it over mine — he's more popular than I am.

PADDY   But he's white — well, off-white.

VAN GOGH   Don't worry, we are going over him with brown ink tonight.

PADDY   Now listen, youse two (*stirs tea with handle of bread-knife*), we all know youse is illegal immigrants. I t'ink you're going to have a lot of trouble with dem two names. Van Gogh and Rembrandt!

LUIGI   They've got trouble with *their* names? What about mine? A coon called Luigi O'Reilly.

PADDY   She shouldn't have left the bedroom door open.

LUIGI   'Oo shouldn't?

ERIC   What 'e's saying is, late one night your mother let in a nigger with a Yorkshire accent.

LUIGI   (*Threatens.*) 'Ere, 'ere, you—

There is a tremendous whip crack sound — then a second.

NEFERTITI   Oh my God, my bra straps have gone.

REMBRANDT   (*Immediately standing up.*) Can I give you a hand?

PADDY   Hand — she needs a bloody shovel!

Nefertiti exits holding bra straps. Sheik Yamani takes curved dagger out of scabbard and starts to slice the bread.

YAMANI   By the sacred word of Allah, I've never heard such terrible abuse heaped upon a fair maiden's head.

REMBRANDT   It wasn't her head.

YAMANI   (*Sticks knife in bread.*) Silence! (*Starts to butter a slice of bread with dagger.*) In my country such an insult to a woman would mean — certain things *cut off*!

PADDY   Like der electricity?

Van Gogh is pouring milk on to his cornflakes. He is pouring it from one of those triangular waxed paper cartons that shoot the milk up in the air.

VAN GOGH   (*Reading milk carton.*) Pure, homogenised, sanferised, pasteurised milk. Keep out of reach of children, must be drunk before November 3rd 1977. I'd better hurry.

SNAP! SNAP!

REMBRANDT   It is the same with food. Last night we are buying three tins of Irish stew, made in Hong Kong.

PADDY.   (*Crossing himself.*) Hong Kong! God forgive them, for they know not what they do!

REMBRANDT   And also on this it says, 'Must be eaten before 4th of June 1937'.

VAN GOGH   Supposing we are putting it in the fridge on November 3rd . . . at one minute past twelve on the morning of the fourth, we go down and open the fridge. What do we see?

PADDY   (*Pointing at Luigi.*) Well, if he's been there first, bugger all.

BLUEY   Why do you drongos waste yer time explaining things to these bloody bungs? These ignorant buggers are best kept in the bloody dark.

VAN GOGH   (*Jumping up.*) We *are* being kept in the bloody dark. There hasn't been a bulb in our room for a month.

PADDY   Well, it's not your turn!

BLUEY   No matter how many lights you put in *his* room he wouldn't be any brighter.

LUIGI   'Ark at this bloody white abo. Have you heard the name of the place he comes from? Wogga Wogga. (*Laughs.*) Wogga Wogga!

BLUEY   Yeah. Bloody Wogga Wogga — that's a dinkum Australian word!

PADDY   Hey all, listen to this. (*Reads from newspaper.*) A Sikh railway porter who has been accused of eating fifty pounds of old *News of the Worlds* said in his defence he ate them after he'd been turned into a goat by the Hindu god Gupta. Is that one of the gods of India?

REMBRANDT   Yes, he is one of them.

PADDY   So he's one of dem as well!

Phone rings.

MUST BE EATEN BEFORE
16 AUG 1983

PADDY   (*Startled*.) Good God, they've connected it again! What bloody fool paid the bill?

NEFERTITI   I did. I have friends even if you don't. (*She picks up phone*.) Shangri-la Boarding House. There's a cheque in the post! (*Long pause while she listens*.) Who is that? (*Another pause then Nefertiti slams the phone down*.)

NEFERTITI   Would you believe it? An obscene phone call at this hour of the morning . . . he was lucky to find me in.

YAMANI   (*Nodding towards Richard*.) You're lucky you're not in his country.

RICHARD   Oh — oh — what's this?

YAMANI   In Israel when they make obscene phone calls they try to reverse the charges.

RICHARD   And in Arabia the women are so ugly they accept them.

YAMANI   Listen you. Underneath the purdah are some of the most beautiful women in the world.

RICHARD   (*Grinning*.) And from what I hear, some of the prettiest men. I mean, we all saw *Lawrence of Arabia*.

YAMANI   Aye, but he couldnae take it. After six months in the desert he had the shakes.

PADDY   And another six months and the bloody sheiks had him.

NEFERTITI   Look, I don't want the subject of homosexuality brought up at this table.

PADDY   But it's the only bloody table we've got.

Nefertiti places a boiled egg in front of Van Gogh. It's in an egg cup covered with a egg cosy.

VAN GOGH   Why is this egg wearing a wig?

NEFERTITI   Wig? That's a cosy.

IF IT WAS AN NHS EGG IT WOULD HAVE FALSE TEETH AS WELL AS A WIG!

VAN GOGH   *(To Rembrandt.)* Do I have to eat it?

REMBRANDT   No, no — that is to keep the egg warm.

VAN GOGH   Why don't they put it under a chicken?

PADDY   Don't be silly. It would look ridiculous to have to crawl under a chicken to eat a boiled egg.

VAN GOGH   Mr Jewboy, why aren't you eating your din-dins?

RICHARD   Oyvez — din-dins. *(Very patiently.)* I am observing Yom Kippur. It's a day of fasting.

PADDY   Don't give us that. His bedroom looks like Tesco's — there's enough salt beef and matzo balls to feed an army.

YAMANI   That's how we got them last time. While they were stuffing themselves with pork sausages we were across the canal.

RICHARD   *(Jumps up.)* Pork? Never! Today is a day for Jewish sacrifice!

VAN GOGH   What are you giving up?

YAMANI   I'll tell ye what he's giving up — the *Jewish Chronicle* and watching that tart across the road in the bath through his binoculars.

VAN GOGH   In our religion the *cow* is a sacred animal. We do not kill them.

BLUEY   You eat 'em *alive*?

REMBRANDT   No, we never eat them. We only use their produce.

VAN GOGH   Like dung.

REMBRANDT   Look, I've just found George Best in my tea.

YAMANI   *(Standing up.)* Well, off to work!

VAN GOGH   What time do you start?

YAMANI   Dead on ten o'clock.

RICHARD   Believe me, he's just as dead at half past.

YAMANI   (*Making gesture of strangulation*.) One day — one day!

RICHARD   It breaks his heart when I go in and cash a cheque on the Bank of Israel!

PADDY   (*Reading paper*.) Here, you was worried about him praying in the wrong direction this morning, wasn't you? It says here on the *Sun* Big Boobs page: 'Miss Eileen Body, voted Miss Bingo, standing outside Brixton *Mecca*.'

Nefertiti leans over his shoulder to take his plate.

VAN GOGH   Mecca is in Brixton now?

PADDY   Yes — like Africa.

✿

Scene 3   *A tatty street. Outside a seedy shop stands a spiv holding a tray. A Union Jack flag hangs down at the front below the words* 'GOD BLESS THE QUEEN'. *The spiv wears an array of medals, all foreign to this country. He is unshaven. On the tray is a collection of cheap glitter jewellery. Pinned on the Union Jack are newspaper cut-outs of the Queen and Prince Philip.*

SPIV   Ex-colonial war hero — help him — God save the Queen lucky charms (*Sings*.) God Save our Queen. Second-hand lucky charms, as worn by Princess Anne. It brought her fame, romance and Mark. Buy one, and marry Prince Andrew. (*Sings*.) God save our gracious Queen. Twenty-five pee or six for thirty pee. Buy while stocks last. God save the Queen. Loverly lucky— (*Stops dead*).

Without looking left or right, he dons black glasses and produces white stick from behind him. He throws a cover over the tray which hangs down over the Union Jack. On it are the words 'Ex-guardsman, wounded at Mons'. *He is holding a begging bowl (a tin mug).*

SPIV   (*Starts to sing*.) Comrades — comrades ever since we were boys —

A policeman enters. He looks into the tin mug, then tips the contents of the mug into his pocket.

POLICEMAN   (*Out of side of mouth.*) Same time tomorrow. (*He saunters off.*)

The spiv stops singing. He lifts his glasses to look after the policeman.

SPIV   (*Whispering.*) Thieving bastard! Coppers are getting too smart. It's 'Police 5' that's doing it . . . Lucky charms — get your lucky— (*He is stopped by the sound of Van Gogh intoning.*)

Van Gogh is kneeling on a prayer mat in front of Mecca Bingo Hall, once a Victorian church. A flashing neon sign proclaims: 'TONIGHT'S GUEST CALLER — BERT WEEDON'.

Rembrandt enters. He is carrying a Union Jack carrier bag and an umbrella.

REMBRANDT   Bapu, I have been looking everywhere for you. Alright — where are your shoes?

VAN GOGH   Perfectiy safe, I left them on a parking meter.

REMBRANDT   You fool, they will be towed away.

VAN GOGH   No, no, I put half an hour on the clock. And the traffic warden only charged me a pound.

❂

Scene 4   *A parking meter on which are parked Van Gogh's shoes. A tramp enters. He is very raggedly dressed and wears boots which are split open at the toes so that the soles flap. One is a white cricketer's boot. The other is a black army boot. The tramp can be heard singing gently as he takes off his boots and swaps them with the pair on the parking meter.*

Scene 5 *Brixton police station. Taffy, a Welsh policeman, is watching TV, from which comes the closing strains of 'Coronation Street'. He gets up and switches off TV.*

TAFFY   You know, Nige, I want to complain about 'Coronation Street'. They don't give the police enough coverage.

NIGE   (*Off, very posh Oxford accent.*) As a whole I find the series incredibly boring and not at all representative of the English people as imagined by Churchill. (*Nigel enters. He is black.*)

Van Gogh and Rembrandt enter and approach the charge desk. Van Gogh is wearing the tramp's boots.

VAN GOGH   Are you nine, nine, nine, Scottish Yard of London?

TAFFY   Can I 'elp you?

REMBRANDT   We wish to report a serious robbery.

Taffy takes out a form and prepares to fill it in. Van Gogh places the tramp's boots — cricket boot and army boot — on the counter. Taffy looks at them from time to time, but makes no comment.

TAFFY   Where did this robbery take place?

VAN GOGH   England. Our home country.

REMBRANDT   E-N-G-L-A-N-

TAFFY   Yes, I know how to spell it. What address?

VAN GOGH   7 Piles Road, Brixton, in England. Our home country. You probably thought we were from Amsterdam.

TAFFY   (*Baffled pause.*) What was the article stolen?

REMBRANDT   One pair of Riviera shoes. (*He is reading from cutting*.) The property of a gentleman. Only done 13,000 miles. Owner going abroad, and— *Taffy grabs cutting from Rembrandt, looks at it, writes on form.*

TAFFY   One pair of shoes... That'll do. Don't tell me you were wearing these shoes when they were stolen?

VAN GOGH   Very well, I won't tell you.

REMBRANDT   And I'll tell you why.

TAFFY   Why?

REMBRANDT   Because he *wasn't* wearing them when they were stolen.

TAFFY   Where were they?

REMBRANDT   In the road.

TAFFY   Why wasn't he in them?

REMBRANDT   Because he wasn't there.

TAFFY   Wasn't there?

VAN GOGH   No, I was outside the Brixton Mecca, praying to Allah.

TAFFY   Were they on a double yellow line?

VAN GOGH   No, they were on a meter.

TAFFY   Had the meter run out?

VAN GOGH   No, that was still there — only the shoes were gone.

Taffy rolls up the form.

AREN'T YOU GOING TO TAKE A DESCRIPTION?

Scene 6 *Paddy's bedroom at No. 7, Piles Road, later the same night. He is asleep in bed. There is a distant sound of a drunken Irishman singing, then a short bleat.*

✿

Scene 7 *The attic room at No. 7, Piles Road. A goat bleats.*

REMBRANDT   Was that you, Bapu?

VAN GOGH   No — it's the goat. Can't you tell the difference?

REMBRANDT   Goat?

VAN GOGH   Yes, I bought a goat — we will get cheap milk.

REMBRANDT   A goat! In here? What about the smell?

VAN GOGH   He'll soon get used to it.

Helpless look comes over Rembrandt's face. The goat bleats.

✿

Scene 8 *Paddy's room. He is dead asleep. The goat bleats twice; at first bleat Paddy's eyes open; at the second he sits up.*

PADDY   (*Crossing himself.*) My God! (*He leaps up and starts to dress.*)

✿

Scene 9 *The street. It is still night. There is heavy rain. Paddy arrives on a bike with a priest on the crossbar and two buckets of holy water on the handlebars.*

PRIEST   Are you quite sure you heard a *goat*?

PADDY   It couldn't have been any other animal.

PRIEST   Ever since I seen Der Exorcist, I been prayin' for dis chance.

Scene 10   *The attic room. The door opens very slowly. The goat bleats.*

PRIEST   (*Whispering.*) Now den, Paddy, I'll hold the crucifix and you t'row de holy water.

They take up a position right where Rembrandt is lying asleep. Priest starts exorcism prayers. The water is thrown over the helpless Van Gogh up on the top bunk. It trickles down onto Rembrandt.

REMBRANDT   (*Sits up.*) You dirty devil!

Lights go on.

PRIEST   Devil? Lord, drive the Protestant devil out of this poor heathen wog.

There is a bleating noise from the cupboard. The priest turns to cupboard and makes the sign of the cross. He pulls open the cupboard door, and stands to one side as he holds the crucifix. Paddy throws a bucket of water square through the cupboard door.

PRIEST   Evil spirit — leave dis home like you done in Der Exorcist.

Goat comes out of cupboard followed by a kid.

PADDY   My God — 'tis a real goat!

PRIEST   Is dis your idea of a joke?

PADDY   (*Kneeling down — crossing himself.*) Farder — forgive, for I have sinned.

As he starts to confess, the kid begins to eat the priest's cassock.